TAX RULES AND PROCEDURE

2018

Revised September 1, 2018

US GOVERNMENT

Table of Contents

TITLE I RULEMAKING AUTHORITY, SCOPE OF RULES, PUBLICATION, CONSTRUCTION, EFFECTIVE DATE, DEFINITIONS

RULE 1. RULEMAKING AUTHORITY, SCOPE OF RULES, PUBLICATION OF RULES AND AMENDMENTS, CONSTRUCTION

(a) Rulemaking Authority: The United States Tax Court, after giving appropriate public notice and an opportunity for comment, may make and amend rules governing its practice and procedure.

(b) Scope of Rules: These Rules govern the practice and procedure in all cases and proceedings before the Court. Where in any instance there is no applicable rule of proce- dure, the Court or the Judge before whom the matter is pending may prescribe the procedure, giving particular weight to the Federal Rules of Civil Procedure to the extent that they are suitably adaptable to govern the matter at hand.

(c) Publication of Rules and Amendments: When new rules or amendments to these Rules are proposed by the Court, notice of such proposals and the ability of the public to comment shall be provided to the Bar and to the general public and shall be posted on the Court's Internet Web site. If the Court determines that there is an immediate need for a particular rule or amendment to an existing rule, it may proceed without public notice and opportunity for comment, but the Court shall promptly thereafter afford such notice and opportunity for comment.

(d) Construction: The Court's Rules shall be construed to secure the just, speedy, and inexpensive determination of every case.

RULE 2. EFFECTIVE DATE

(a) Adoption: These Rules, except as otherwise provided, are effective as of October 3, 2008. They govern all proceedings and cases commenced after they take effect, andalso all further proceedings in cases then pending, except to the extent that in the opinion of the Court their application, in a particular case pending when the Rules take effect, would not be feasible or would work injustice, in which event the former procedure applies.

(b) Amendments: Amendments to these Rules shall state their effective date. Amendments shall likewise govern all proceedings both in cases pending on or commenced after their effective date, except to the extent otherwise provided, and subject to the further exception provided in paragraph (a) of this Rule.

RULE 3. DEFINITIONS

(a) Division: The Chief Judge may from time to time divide the Court into Divisions of one or more Judges and, in case of a Division of more than one Judge, designate the chief thereof.

(b) Clerk: Reference to the Clerk in these Rules means the Clerk of the United States Tax Court.

(c) Commissioner: Reference to the Commissioner in these Rules means the Commissioner of Internal Revenue.

(d) Special Trial Judge: The term Special Trial Judge as used in these Rules refers to a judicial officer appointed pursuant to Code section 7443A(a). See Rule 180.

(e) Time: As provided in these Rules and in orders and notices of the Court, time means standard time in the location mentioned except when advanced time is substituted therefor by law. For computation of time, see Rule 25.

(f) Business Hours: As to the Court's business hours, see Rule 10(d).

(g) Filing: For requirements as to filing with the Court, see Rule 22.

(h) Code: Any reference or citation to the Code relates to the Internal Revenue Code of 1986, as in effect for the relevant period or the relevant time.

TITLE II THE COURT

RULE 10. NAME, OFFICE, AND SESSIONS

(a) Name: The name of the Court is the United States Tax Court.

(b) Office of the Court: The principal office of the Court shall be in the District of Columbia, but the Court or any of its Divisions may sit at any place within the United States. See Code secs. 7445, 7701(a)(9).

(c) Sessions: The time and place of sessions of the Court shall be prescribed by the Chief Judge.

[1]**(d) Business Hours:** The office of the Clerk at Washington, D.C., shall be open during business hours on all days, except Saturdays, Sundays, and Federal holidays, for the purpose of receiving petitions, pleadings, motions, and other papers. Business hours are from 8 a.m. to 4:30 p.m.

(e) Mailing Address: Mail to the Court should be addressed to the United States Tax Court, 400 Second Street, N.W., Washington, D.C. 20217. Other addresses, such as locations at which the Court may be in session, should not be used, unless the Court directs otherwise.

RULE 11. PAYMENTS TO THE COURT [2]

All payments to the Court for fees or charges of the Court shall be made either in cash or by check, money order, or other draft made payable to the order of ''Clerk, United States Tax Court'', and shall be mailed or delivered to the Clerk of the Court at Washington, D.C. The Court may also permit specified fees or charges to be paid by credit card. For the Court's address, see Rule 10(e). For particular payments, see Rules 12(c) (copies of Court records), 20(d) (filing of peti- tion), 173(a)(2) (small tax cases), 200(a) (application to prac- tice before Court), 200(g) (periodic registration fee), 271(c) (filing of petition for administrative costs), 281(c) (filing of petition for review of failure to abate interest), 291(d) (filing of petition for redetermination of employment status), 311(c) (filing of petition for declaratory judgment relating to treat- ment of items other than partnership items with respect to an oversheltered return), 321(d) (filing of petition for deter- mination of relief from joint and several liability on a joint return), 331(d) (filing of petition for lien and levy action), and 341(c) (filing of petition for whistleblower action). For fees and charges payable to the Court, see Appendix II.

RULE 12. COURT RECORDS

[1](a) **Removal of Records:** No original record, paper, document, or exhibit filed with the Court shall be taken from the courtroom, from the offices of the Court, or from the cus- tody of a Judge, a Special Trial Judge, or an employee of the Court, except as authorized by a Judge or Special Trial Judge of the Court or except as may be necessary for the Clerk to furnish copies or to transmit the same to other courts for appeal or other official purposes. With respect to return of exhibits after a decision of the Court becomes final, see Rule 143(e)(2).

(b) Copies of Records: After the Court renders its de- cision in a case, a plain or certified copy of any document, record, entry, or other paper, pertaining to the case and still in the custody of the Court, may be obtained upon applica- tion to the Court's Copywork Office and payment of the re- quired fee. Unless otherwise permitted by the Court, no copy of any exhibit or original document in the files of the Court shall be furnished to other than the parties until the Court renders its decision. With respect to protective orders that may restrict the availability of exhibits and documents, see Code section 7461 and Rule 103(a).

(c) Fees: The fees to be charged and collected for any copies will be determined in accordance with Code section 7474. See Appendix II.

(d)

13

RULE 13. JURISDICTION

(a) Notice of Deficiency or of Transferee or Fiduciary Liability Required: Except in actions for declaratory judgment, for disclosure, for readjustment or adjustment of partnership items, for administrative costs, for review of failure to abate interest, for redetermination of employment status, for determination of relief from joint and several liability, for lien and levy, or for review of whistleblower awards (see Titles XXI, XXII, XXIV, and XXVI through XXXIII), the jurisdiction of the Court depends: (1) In a case commenced in the Court by a taxpayer, upon the issuance by the Commissioner of a notice of deficiency in income, gift, or estate tax or, in the taxes under Code chapter 41, 42, 43, or 44 (relating to the excise taxes on certain organizations and persons dealing with them), or in the tax under Code chapter 45 (relating to the windfall profit tax), or in any other taxes which are the subject of the issuance of a notice of deficiency by the Commissioner; and (2) in a case commenced in the Court by a transferee or fiduciary, upon the issuance by the Commissioner of a notice of liability to the transferee or fiduciary. See Code secs. 6212, 6213, 6901.

(b) Declaratory Judgment, Disclosure, Partnership, Administrative Costs, Review of Failure To Abate Interest, Redetermination of Employment Status, Determination of Relief From Joint and Several Liability, Lien and Levy, or Whistleblower Action: For the jurisdictional requirements in an action for declaratory judgment, for disclosure, for readjustment or adjustment of partnership items, for administrative costs, for review of failure to abate interest, for redetermination of employment status, for determination of relief from joint and several liability, for lien and levy, or for review of whistleblower awards, see Rules 210(c), 220(c), 240(c), 270(c), 280(b), 290(b), 300(c), 310(c), 320(b), 330(b), and 340(b), respectively.

(c) Timely Petition Required: In all cases, the jurisdiction of the Court also depends on the timely filing of a petition. See Code sections 6213 and 7502; with respect to administrative costs actions, see Code section 7430(f); with respect to declaratory judgment actions, see Code sections 6234, 7428, 7476, 7477, 7478, and 7479; with respect to determination of relief from joint and liability actions, see Code section 6015(e); with respect to disclosure actions, see Code section 6110; with respect to lien and levy actions, see Code sections 6320 and 6330; with respect to partnership actions, see Code sections 6226, 6228, and 6247; with respect to rede- termination of employment status actions, see Code section 7436; with respect to review of failure to abate interest ac- tions, see Code section 6404(h); and with respect to whistleblower actions, see Code section 7623(b)(4).

(d) Contempt of Court: Contempt of Court may be

punished by fine or imprisonment within the scope of Code section 7456(c).

(e) Bankruptcy and Receivership: With respect to the filing of a petition or the continuation of proceedings in this Court after the filing of a bankruptcy petition, see 11 U.S.C. section 362(a)(8) and Code section 6213(f)(1). With respect to the filing of a petition in this Court after the appointment of a receiver in a receivership proceeding, see Code section 6871(c)(2).

TITLE III COMMENCEMENT OF CASE, SERVICE AND FILING OF PAPERS, FORM AND STYLE OF PAPERS, APPEARANCE AND REPRESENTATION, COMPUTATION OF TIME

RULE 20. COMMENCEMENT OF CASE

(a) General: A case is commenced in the Court by filing a petition with the Court, inter alia, to redetermine a deficiency set forth in a notice of deficiency issued by the Com- missioner, or to redetermine the liability of a transferee or fiduciary set forth in a notice of liability issued by the Com- missioner to the transferee or fiduciary, or to obtain a declar- atory judgment, or to obtain or restrain a disclosure, or to ad- just or readjust partnership items, or to obtain an award for reasonable administrative costs, or to obtain a review of the Commissioner's failure to abate interest. See Rule 13.

(b) Statement of Taxpayer Identification Number: The petitioner shall submit with the petition a statement of the petitioner's taxpayer identification number (e.g., Social Security number or employer identification number), or lack thereof. The statement shall be substantially in accordance with Form 4 shown in Appendix I.

[1]**(c) Disclosure Statement:** A nongovernmental cor- poration, large partnership, or limited liability company, or a tax matters partner or partner other than the tax matters partner of a nongovernmental partnership filing a petition with the Court shall file with the petition a separate disclo- sure statement. In the case of a nongovernmental corpora- tion, the disclosure statement shall identify any parent cor- poration and any publicly held entity owning 10 percent or more of petitioner's stock or state that there is no such enti- ty. In the case of a nongovernmental large partnership or limited liability company, or a tax matters partner or partner other than a tax matters partner of a nongovernmental part- nership, the disclosure statement shall identify any publicly held entity owning an interest in the large partnership, the limited liability company, or the partnership, or state that there is no such entity. A petitioner shall promptly file a sup- plemental statement if there is any change in the informa- tion required under this rule. For the form of such disclosure

statement, see Form 6, Appendix I. For the definition of a large partnership, see Rule 300(b)(1). For the definitions of a partnership and a tax matters partner, see Rule 240(b)(1), (4). A partner other than a tax matters partner is a notice partner or a 5-percent group as defined in Rule 240(b)(8) and (9).

[1](d) **Filing Fee:** At the time of filing a petition, a fee of $60 shall be paid. The payment of any fee under this para- graph may be waived if the petitioner establishes to the sat- isfaction of the Court by an affidavit or a declaration con- taining specific financial information the inability to make such payment.

RULE 21. SERVICE OF PAPERS

(a) When Required: Except as otherwise required by these Rules or directed by the Court, all pleadings, motions, orders, decisions, notices, demands, briefs, appearances, or other similar documents or papers relating to a case, includ- ing a disciplinary matter under Rule 202, also referred to as the papers in a case, shall be served on each of the parties or other persons involved in the matter to which the paper relates other than the party who filed the paper.

[2](b) **Manner of Service:** (1) *General:* All petitions shall be served by the Clerk. Unless otherwise provided in these Rules or directed by the Court, all other papers re- quired to be served on a party shall be served by the party filing the paper, and the original paper shall be filed with a certificate by a party or a party's counsel that service of that paper has been made on the party to be served or such par- ty's counsel. For the form of such certificate of service, see Form 9, Appendix I. Such service may be made by:

(A) Mail directed to the party or the party's counsel at such person's last known address. Service by mail is complete upon mailing, and the date of such mailing shall be the date of such service.

(B) Delivery to a party, or a party's counsel or au- thorized representative in the case of a party other than an individual (see Rule 24(b)).

(C) Mail directed or delivery to the Commissioner's counsel at the office address shown in the Commis- sioner's answer filed in the case or a motion filed in lieu   of an answer. If no answer or motion in lieu of an an- swer has been filed, then mail shall be directed or deliv- ered to the Chief Counsel, Internal Revenue Service, Washington, D.C. 20224.

(D) Electronic means if the person served consented in writing, in which event service is complete upon transmission, but is not effective if the serving party learns that it did not reach the person to be served.

Service on a person other than a party shall be made in the same manner as service on a party, except as otherwise pro- vided in these Rules or directed by the Court. In cases con- solidated pursuant to Rule 141, a party making service of a paper shall serve each of the other parties or counsel for each of the other parties, and the original and copies thereof re- quired to be filed with the Court shall each have a certificate of service attached.

(2) *Counsel of Record:* Whenever under these Rules service is required or permitted to be made upon a party represented by counsel who has entered an appearance, service shall be made upon such counsel unless service upon the party is directed by the Court. Where more than one counsel appear for a party, service is required to be made only on that counsel whose appearance was first en- tered of record, unless that counsel notifies the Court, by a designation of counsel to receive service filed with the Court, that other counsel of record is to receive service, in which event service is required to be made only on the per- son so designated.

(3) *Writs and Process:* Service and execution of writs, process, or similar directives of the Court may be made by a United States marshal, by a deputy marshal, or by a per- son specially appointed by the Court for that purpose, except that a subpoena may be served as provided in Rule 147(c). The person making service shall make proof thereof to the Court promptly and in any event within the time in which the person served must respond. Failure to make proof of service does not affect the validity of the service.

(4) *Change of Address:* The Court shall be promptly notified, by a notice of change of address filed with the Court, of the change of mailing address of any party, any party's counsel, or any party's duly authorized representa- tive in the case of a party other than an individual (see Rule 24(a)(2), (a)(3), (b), and (d)). A separate notice of change of address shall be filed for each docket number. For the form of such notice of change of address, see Form 10 in Appendix I.

(5) *Using Court Transmission Facilities:* A party may make service under Rule 21(b)(1)(D) through the Court's transmission facilities pursuant to electronic service proce- dures prescribed by the Court.

RULE 22. FILING[1]

Any pleadings or other papers to be filed with the Court must be filed with the Clerk in Washington, D.C., during business hours, except that the Judge or Special Trial Judge presiding at any trial or hearing may permit or require docu- ments pertaining thereto to be filed at that particular session of the Court, or except as otherwise directed by the Court. For the circumstances under which timely mailed papers will be treated as having been timely filed, see Code section 7502.

RULE 23. FORM AND STYLE OF PAPERS

(a) Caption, Date, and Signature Required: All papers filed with the Court shall have a caption, shall be dated, and shall be signed as follows:

(1) *Caption:* A proper caption shall be placed on all papers filed with the Court, and the requirements provided in Rule 32(a) shall be satisfied with respect to all such papers. All prefixes and titles, such as ''Mr.'', ''Ms.'', or ''Dr.'', shall be omitted from the caption. The full name and surname of each individual petitioner shall be set forth in the caption. The name of an estate or trust or other person for whom a fiduciary acts shall precede the fiduciary's name and title, as for example ''Estate of Mary Doe, Deceased, Richard Roe, Executor''.

(2) *Date:* The date of signature shall be placed on all papers filed with the Court.

(3) *Signature:* The original signature, either of the party or the party's counsel, shall be subscribed in writing to the original of every paper filed by or for that party with the Court, except as otherwise provided by these Rules. An individual rather than a firm name shall be used, except that the signature of a petitioner corporation or unincorporated association shall be in the name of the corporation or association by one of its active and authorized officers or members, as for example ''Mary Doe, Inc., by Richard Roe, President''. The name, mailing address, and telephone number of the party or the party's counsel, as well as counsel's Tax Court bar number, shall be typed or printed immediately beneath the written signature. The mailing address of a signatory shall include a firm name if it is an essential part of the accurate mailing address.

[1]**(b) Number Filed:** For each document filed in paper form, there shall be filed the signed original and one conformed copy, except as otherwise provided in these Rules. Where filing is in more than one case (as a motion to consolidate, or in cases already consolidated), the number filed shall include one additional copy for each docket number in excess of one. If service of a paper is to be made by the Clerk, copies of any attachments to the original of such paper shall be attached to each copy to be served by the Clerk. As to stipulations, see Rule 91(b).

(c) Legible Papers Required: Papers filed with the Court may be prepared by any process, but only if all papers, including copies, filed with the Court are clear and legible.

[2]**(d) Size and Style:** Typewritten or printed papers shall be typed or printed only on one side, on opaque, unglazed paper, 8½ inches wide by 11 inches long. All such papers shall have margins on both sides of each page that are no less than 1 inch wide, and margins on the top and bottom of each page that are no less than ¾ inch wide. Text and footnotes shall appear in consistent typeface no smaller

than 12 characters per inch produced by a typewriting element, 12-point type produced by a nonproportional print font (e.g., Courier), or 14-point type produced by a proportional print font (e.g., Times New Roman), with double spacing be- tween each line of text and single spacing between each line of indented quotations and footnotes. Quotations in excess of five lines shall be set off from the surrounding text and in- dented. Double-spaced lines shall be no more than three lines to the vertical inch, and single-spaced lines shall be no more than six lines to the vertical inch.

(e) Binding and Covers: All papers shall be bound together on the upper left-hand side only and shall have no backs or covers.

(f) Citations: All citations of case names shall be underscored when typewritten, and shall be in italic when printed.

[1]**(g) Acceptance by the Clerk:** Except as otherwise directed by the Court, the Clerk must not refuse to file a paper solely because it is not in the form prescribed by these Rules.

RULE 24. APPEARANCE AND REPRESENTATION

(a) Appearance: (1) *General:* Counsel may enter an appearance either by subscribing the petition or other initial pleading or document in accordance with subparagraph (2) hereof, or thereafter by filing an entry of appearance in accordance with subparagraph (3) hereof or, in a case not calendared for trial or hearing, a substitution of counsel in accordance with paragraph (d) hereof.

(2) *Appearance in Initial Pleading:* If (A) the petition or other paper initiating the participation of a party in a case is subscribed by counsel admitted to practice before the Court, and (B) such initial paper contains the mailing address and Tax Court bar number of counsel and other information required for entry of appearance (see subparagraph (3)), then (C) that counsel shall be recognized as representing that party and no separate entry of appearance shall be necessary. Thereafter counsel shall be required to notify the Clerk of any changes in applicable information to the same extent as if counsel had filed a separate entry of appearance.

Subsequent Appearance: Where counsel has not previously appeared, counsel shall file an entry of appearance in duplicate, signed by counsel individually, containing the name and docket number of the case, the name, mailing address, telephone number, and Tax Court bar number of counsel so appearing, and a statement that counsel is admitted to practice before the Court. A separate entry of appearance, in duplicate, shall be filed for each additional docket number in which counsel shall appear. The entry of appearance shall be substantially in the form set forth in Form 7 in Appendix I. The Clerk shall be given prompt written notice, filed in duplicate for each docket number, of any change in the foregoing information.

(3) *Counsel Not Admitted to Practice:* No entry of appearance by counsel not admitted to practice before this Court will be effective until counsel shall have been admitted, but counsel may be recognized as counsel in a pending case to the extent permitted by the Court and then only where it appears that counsel can and will be promptly ad- mitted. For the procedure for admission to practice before the Court, see Rule 200.

[1](5) *Law Student Assistance:* With the permission of the presiding Judge or Special Trial Judge, and under the direct supervision of counsel in a case, a law student may assist such counsel by presenting all or any part of the par- ty's case at a hearing or trial. In addition, a law student may assist counsel in a case in drafting a pleading or other document to be filed with the Court. A law student may not, however, enter an appearance in any case, be recog- nized as counsel in a case, or sign a pleading or other docu- ment filed with the Court. The Court may acknowledge the law student assistance.

(b) Personal Representation Without Counsel: In the absence of appearance by counsel, a party will be deemed to appear on the party's own behalf. An individual party may represent himself or herself. A corporation or an unincor- porated association may be represented by an authorized offi- cer of the corporation or by an authorized member of the as- sociation. An estate or trust may be represented by a fidu- ciary thereof. Any such person shall state, in the initialpleading or other paper filed by or for the party, such per- son's name, address, and telephone number, and thereafter shall promptly notify the Clerk in writing, in duplicate for each docket number involving that party, of any change in that information.

(c) Withdrawal of Counsel: Counsel of record desiring to withdraw such counsel's appearance, or any party desiring to withdraw the appearance of counsel of record for such party, must file a motion with the Court requesting leave therefor, showing that prior notice of the motion has been given by such counsel to such counsel's client, or such party's counsel, as the case may be, and to each of the other parties to the case or their counsel, and stating whether there is any objection to the motion. A motion to withdraw as counsel and a motion to withdraw counsel shall each also state the then- current mailing address and telephone number of the party in respect of whom or by whom the motion is filed. The Court may, in its discretion, deny such motion.

(d) Substitution of Counsel: In a case not calendared for trial or hearing, counsel of record for a party may with- draw such counsel's appearance, and counsel who has not previously appeared may enter an appearance, by filing a substitution of counsel, showing that prior notice of the sub- stitution has been given by counsel of record to such coun- sel's client, and to each of the other parties to the case or their counsel, and that there is no objection to the substi- tution. The substitution of counsel shall be signed by counsel of record and substituted counsel individually, and shall con- tain the information required by subparagraph (3) of para- graph (a). The substitution of counsel shall be substantially in the form set forth in Form 8 in Appendix I. Thereafter substituted counsel shall be required to notify the Clerk of any changes in applicable information to the same extent as if such counsel had filed a separate entry of appearance.

(e) Death of Counsel: If counsel of record dies, the Court shall be so notified, and other counsel may enter an appearance in accordance with this Rule.

[1]**(f) Change in Party or Authorized Representative or Fiduciary:** Where (1) a party other than an individual participates in a case through an authorized representative (such as an officer of a corporation or a member of an asso- ciation) or through a fiduciary, and there is a change in such representative or fiduciary, or (2) there is a substitution of parties in a pending case, counsel subscribing the motion re- sulting in the Court's approval of the change or substitution shall thereafter be deemed first counsel of record for the rep- resentative, fiduciary, or party. Counsel of record for the former representative, fiduciary, or party, desiring to with- draw such counsel's appearance shall file a motion in accord- ance with paragraph (c).

(g) Conflict of Interest: If any counsel of record (1) was involved in planning or promoting a transaction or oper- ating an entity that is connected to any issue in a case, (2) represents more than one person with differing interests with respect to any issue in a case, or (3) is a potential wit- ness in a case, then such counsel must either secure the in- formed consent of the client (but only as to items (1) and (2)); withdraw from the case; or take whatever other steps are necessary to obviate a conflict of interest or other violation of the ABA Model Rules of Professional Conduct, and par- ticularly rules 1.7, 1.8, and 3.7 thereof. The Court may in- quire into the circumstances of counsel's employment in order to deter such violations. See

RULE 25. COMPUTATION OF TIME

(a) Computation: (1) *General:* In computing any pe- riod of time prescribed or allowed by these Rules or by direc- tion of the Court or by any applicable statute which does not provide otherwise, the day of the act, event, or default from which a designated period of time begins to run shall not be included, and (except as provided in subparagraph (2)) the last day of the period so computed shall be included. If serv- ice is made by mail, then a period of time computed with re- spect to the service shall begin on the day after the date of mailing.

(2) *Saturdays, Sundays, and Holidays:* Saturdays, Sundays, and all legal holidays shall be counted, except that, (A) if the period prescribed or allowed is less than 7 days, then intermediate Saturdays, Sundays, and legal holidays in

the District of Columbia shall be excluded in the computation; (B) if the last day of the period so com- puted is a Saturday, Sunday, or a legal holiday in the Dis- trict of Columbia, then that day shall not be included and the period shall run until the end of the next day which is not a Saturday, Sunday, or such a legal holiday; and (C) if any act is required to be taken or completed no later than (or at least) a specified number of days before a date certain, then the earliest day of the period so specified shall not be included if it is a Saturday, Sunday, or a legal holiday in the District of Columbia, and the earliest such day shall be the next preceding day which is not a Satur- day, Sunday, or such a legal holiday. When such a legal holiday falls on a Sunday, the next day shall be considered a holiday; and, when such a legal holiday falls on a Satur- day, the preceding day shall be considered a holiday.

(3) *Cross-References:* For computation of the period within which to file a petition with the Court to redeter- mine a deficiency or liability, see Code section 6213; for the period within which to file a petition in an action for deter- mination of relief from joint and several liability, see Code section 6015(e); for the period within which to file a peti- tion in a disclosure action, see Code section 6110; for the period within which to file a petition in a declaratory judg- ment action, see Code sections 6234, 7428, 7476, 7477, 7478, and 7479; for the period within which to file a peti- tion in a partnership action, see Code sections 6226, 6228, and 6247; for the period within which to file a petition for a lien or levy action, see Code sections 6320 and 6330; for the period within which to file a petition in a review of fail- ure to abate interest action, see Code section 6404(h); for the period within which to file a petition in an administra- tive costs action, see Code section 7430(f); for the period within which to file a petition in a redetermination of em- ployment status action, see Code section 7436; and for the period within which to file a petition in a whistleblower ac- tion, see Code section 7623(b). See also Code sec. 7502.

(b) District of Columbia Legal Holidays: The legal holidays within the District of Columbia, in addition to any other day appointed as a holiday by the President or the Congress of the United States, are as follows:

New Year's Day—January 1
Birthday of Martin Luther King, Jr.—Third Monday in January
Inauguration Day—Every fourth year
Washington's Birthday—Third Monday in February
District of Columbia Emancipation Day—April 16
Memorial Day—Last Monday in May
Independence Day—July 4
Labor Day—First Monday in September
Columbus Day—Second Monday in October
Veterans Day—November 11
Thanksgiving Day—Fourth Thursday in November

(c) **Enlargement or Reduction of Time:** Unless precluded by statute, the Court in its discretion may make longer or shorter any period provided by these Rules. As to continuances, see Rule 133. Where a motion is made concerning jurisdiction or the sufficiency of a pleading, the time for filing a response to that pleading shall begin to run from the date of service of the order disposing of the motion by the Court, unless the Court shall direct otherwise. Where the dates for filing briefs are fixed, an extension of time for filing a brief or the granting of leave to file a brief after the due date shall correspondingly extend the time for filing any other brief due at the same time and for filing succeeding briefs, unless the Court shall order otherwise. The period fixed by statute, within which to file a petition with the Court, cannot be extended by the Court.

(d) **Miscellaneous:** With respect to the computation of time, see also Rule 3(e) (definition), Rule 10(d) (business hours of the Court), Rule 13(c) (filing of petition), and Rule 133 (continuances).

RULE 26. ELECTRONIC FILING [1]

(a) **General:** The Court will accept for filing papers submitted, signed, or verified by electronic means that com- ply with procedures established by the Court. A paper filed electronically in compliance with the Court's electronic filing procedures is a written paper for purposes of these Rules.

(b) **Electronic Filing Requirement:** Electronic filing is required for all papers filed by parties represented by counsel in open cases. Mandatory electronic filing does not apply to:

(1) petitions and other papers not eligible for electronic filing in the Court (for a complete list of those papers, see the Court's eFiling Instructions on the Court's Web site at www.ustaxcourt.gov);

(2) self-represented petitioners, including petitioners assisted by low-income taxpayer clinics and Bar-sponsored pro bono programs; and

(3) any counsel in a case who, upon motion filed in paper form and for good cause shown, is granted an excep- tion from the electronic filing requirement. Because a mo- tion for exception does not extend any period provided by these Rules, the motion shall be accompanied by any docu- ment sought to be filed in paper form.

RULE 27. PRIVACY PROTECTION FOR FILINGS MADE WITH THE COURT

(a) **Redacted Filings:** Except as otherwise required by these Rules or directed by the Court, in an electronic or paper filing with the Court, a party or nonparty making the filing should refrain from including or should take appro- priate steps to redact the following information:

(1) Taxpayer identification numbers (e.g., Social Secu- rity numbers or employer identification numbers).

(2) Dates of birth. If a date of birth is provided, only the year should appear.

(3) Names of minor children. If a minor child is identi- fied, only the minor child's initials should appear.

(4) Financial account numbers. If a financial account number is provided, only the last four digits of the number should appear.

(b) Limitations on Remote Access to Electronic Files: Except as otherwise directed by the Court, access to an electronic file is authorized as follows:

(1) The parties and their counsel may have remote elec- tronic access to any part of the case file maintained by the Court in electronic form; and

(2) any other person may have electronic access at the courthouse to the public record maintained by the Court in electronic form, but may have remote electronic access only to:

(A) The docket record maintained by the Court; and

(B) any opinion, order, or decision of the Court, but not any other part of the case file.

(c) Filings Made Under Seal: The Court may order that a filing containing any of the information described in paragraph (a) of this Rule be made under seal without redac- tion. The Court may later unseal the filing or order the per- son who made the filing to file a redacted version for the public record.

(d) Protective Orders: For good cause, the Court may by order in a case:

(1) Require redaction of additional information; or

(2) issue a protective order as provided by Rule 103(a).

(e) Option for Additional Unredacted Filing Under Seal: A person making a redacted filing may also file an unredacted copy under seal. The Court must retain the unredacted copy as part of the record.

(f) Option for Filing a Reference List: A document that contains redacted information may be filed together with a reference list that identifies each item of redacted in- formation and specifies an appropriate identifier that unique- ly corresponds to each item listed. The list must be filed with a motion to seal and may be amended as of right. Any ref- erence in the case to a listed identifier will be construed to refer to the corresponding item of information.

(g) Waiver of Protection of Identifiers: A person waives the protection of this Rule as to the person's own in- formation by filing it without redaction and not under seal. The

24

Clerk of the Court is not required to review documents filed with the Court for compliance with this Rule. The responsibility to redact a filing rests with the party or nonparty making the filing.

(h) Inadvertent Waiver: A party may correct an inadvertent disclosure of identifying information in a prior filing by submitting a properly redacted substitute filing within 60 days of the original filing without leave of Court, and there- after only by leave of Court.

TITLE IV PLEADINGS

RULE 30. PLEADINGS ALLOWED

There shall be a petition and an answer, and, where re- quired under these Rules, a reply. No other pleading shall be allowed, except that the Court may permit or direct some other responsive pleading. (See Rule 173 as to small tax cases.)

RULE 31. GENERAL RULES OF PLEADING

(a) Purpose: The purpose of the pleadings is to give the parties and the Court fair notice of the matters in con- troversy and the basis for their respective positions.

(b) Pleading To Be Concise and Direct: Each aver- ment of a pleading shall be simple, concise, and direct. No technical forms of pleading are required.

(c) Consistency: A party may set forth two or more statements of a claim or defense alternatively or hypo- thetically. When two or more statements are made in the al- ternative and one of them would be sufficient if made inde- pendently, the pleading is not made insufficient by the insuf- ficiency of one or more of the alternative statements. A party may state as many separate claims or defenses as the party has regardless of consistency or the grounds on which based. All statements shall be made subject to the signature re- quirements of Rules 23(a)(3) and 33.

(d) Construction of Pleadings: All pleadings shall be so construed as to do substantial justice.

RULE 32. FORM OF PLEADINGS

(a) Caption; Names of Parties: Every pleading shall contain a caption setting forth the name of the Court (United States Tax Court), the title of the case, the docket number after it becomes available (see Rule 35), and a designation to show the nature of the pleading. In the petition, the title of the case shall include the names of all parties, but shall not include as a party-petitioner the name of any person other than the person or persons by or on whose behalf the petition is filed. In other pleadings, it is sufficient to state the name of the first party with an appropriate indication of other parties.

(b) Separate Statement: All averments of claim or defense, and all statements in support thereof, shall be made   in separately designated paragraphs, the contents of each of which shall be limited as far as practicable to a statement of   a single item or a single set of circumstances. Such para- graph may be referred to by that designation in all suc- ceeding pleadings. Each claim and defense shall be stated separately whenever a separation facilitates the clear presen- tation of the matters set forth.

(c) Adoption by Reference; Exhibits: Statements in a pleading may be adopted by reference in a different part   of the same pleading or in another pleading or in any motion. A copy of any written instrument which is an exhibit to a pleading is a part thereof for all purposes.

(d) Other Provisions: With respect to other provisions relating to the form and style of papers filed with the Court, see Rules 23, 56(a), 57(a), 210(d), 220(d), 240(d), 300(d), and 320(c).

RULE 33. SIGNING OF PLEADINGS

[1]**(a) Signature:** Each pleading shall be signed in the manner provided in Rule 23. Where there is more than one attorney of record, the signature of only one is required. Ex-   cept when otherwise specifically directed by the Court, plead- ings need not be verified or accompanied by affidavit or dec- laration.

(b) Effect of Signature: The signature of counsel or a party constitutes a certificate by the signer that the signer has read the pleading; that, to the best of the signer's knowl- edge, information, and belief formed after reasonable inquiry, it is well grounded in fact and is warranted by existing law or a good faith argument for the extension, modification, or reversal of existing law; and that it is not interposed for any improper purpose, such as to harass or to cause unnecessary delay or needless increase in the cost of litigation. The signa- ture of counsel also constitutes a representation by counsel that counsel is authorized to represent the party or parties on whose behalf the pleading is filed. If a pleading is not signed, it shall be stricken, unless it is signed promptly after the omission is called to the attention of the pleader. If a pleading is signed in violation of this Rule, the Court, upon motion or upon its own initiative, may impose upon the per- son who signed it, a represented party, or both, an appro- priate sanction, which may include an order to pay to the other party or parties the amount of the reasonable expenses incurred because of the filing of the pleading, including rea- sonable counsel's fees.

RULE 34. PETITION

(a) General: (1) *Deficiency or Liability Action:* The

petition with respect to a notice of deficiency or a notice of liability shall be substantially in accordance with Form 1 shown in Appendix I, and shall comply with the requirements of these Rules relating to pleadings. Ordinarily, a separate petition shall be filed with respect to each notice of deficiency or each notice of liability. However, a single petition may be filed seeking a redetermination with respect to all notices of deficiency or liability directed to one person alone or to such person and one or more other persons or to a husband and a wife individually, except that the Court may require a severance and a separate case to be maintained with respect to one or more of such notices. Where the notice of deficiency or liability is directed to more than one person, each such person desiring to contest it shall file a petition, either separately or jointly with any such other person, and each such person must satisfy all the requirements of this Rule in order for the petition to be treated as filed by or for such person. The petition shall be complete, so as to enable ascertainment of the issues intended to be presented. No telegram, cablegram, radiogram, telephone call, electronically transmitted copy, or similar communication will be recognized as a petition. Failure of the petition to satisfy applicable requirements may be ground for dismissal of the case. As to the joinder of parties, see Rule 61; and as to the effect of misjoinder of parties, see Rule 62. For the circumstances under which a timely mailed petition will be treated as having been timely filed, see Code section 7502.

(2) *Other Actions:* For the requirements relating to the petitions in other actions, see the following Rules: Declaratory judgment actions, Rules 211(b), 311(b); disclosure actions, Rule 221(b); partnership actions, Rules 241(b), 301(b); administrative costs actions, Rule 271(b); abatement of interest actions, Rule 281(b); redetermination of employment status actions, Rule 291(b); determination of relief from joint and several liability on a joint return actions, Rule 321(b); lien and levy actions, Rule 331(b); and whistleblower actions, Rule 341(b). As to joinder of parties in declaratory judgment actions, in disclosure actions, and in partnership actions, see Rules 215, 226, and 241(h) and 301(f), respectively.

(b) Content of Petition in Deficiency or Liability Action: The petition in a deficiency or liability action shall contain (see Form 1, Appendix I):

(1) In the case of a petitioner who is an individual, the petitioner's name and State of legal residence; in the case of a petitioner other than an individual, the petitioner's name and principal place of business or principal office or agency; and, in all cases, the petitioner's mailing address and the office of the Internal Revenue Service with which the tax return for the period in controversy was filed. The mailing address, State of legal residence, principal place of business,

or principal office or agency shall be stated as of the date of filing the petition. In the event of a variance between the name set forth in the notice of deficiency or liability and the correct name, a statement of the reasons for such variance shall be set forth in the petition.

(2) The date of the notice of deficiency or liability, or other proper allegations showing jurisdiction in the Court, and the City and State of the office of the Internal Rev- enue Service which issued the notice.

(3) The amount of the deficiency or liability, as the case may be, determined by the Commissioner, the nature of the tax, the year or years or other periods for which the determination was made; and, if different from the Commissioner's determination, the approximate amount of taxes in controversy.
Clear and concise assignments of each and every error which the petitioner alleges to have been committed by the Commissioner in the determination of the deficiency or liability. The assignments of error shall include issues in respect of which the burden of proof is on the Commissioner. Any issue not raised in the assignments of error shall be deemed to be conceded. Each assignment of error shall be separately lettered.

(4) Clear and concise lettered statements of the facts on which petitioner bases the assignments of error, except with respect to those assignments of error as to which the burden of proof is on the Commissioner.

(5) A prayer setting forth relief sought by the petitioner.

(6) The signature, mailing address, and telephone number of each petitioner or each petitioner's counsel, as well as counsel's Tax Court bar number.

(7) A copy of the notice of deficiency or liability, as the case may be, which shall be appended to the petition, and with which there shall be included so much of any state- ment accompanying the notice as is material to the issues raised by the assignments of error. If the notice of defi- ciency or liability or accompanying statement incorporates by reference any prior notices, or other material furnished by the Internal Revenue Service, such parts thereof as are material to the issues raised by the assignments of error likewise shall be appended to the petition.
A claim for reasonable litigation or administrative costs shall not be included in the petition in a deficiency or liability action. For the requirements as to claims for reasonable litigation or administrative costs, see Rule 231.

(c) Content of Petition in Other Actions: For the requirements as to the content of the petition in a small tax case, see Rule 173(a). For the requirements as to the content of the petition in other actions, see Rule 211(c), (d), (e), (f), and (g), Rule 221(c), (d), and (e), Rule 241(c), (d), and (e), Rule 271(b), Rule 281(b), Rule 291(b), Rule 301(b), Rule

311(b), Rule 321(b), Rule 331(b), and Rule 341(b).

(d) Use of Form 2 Petition: The use of a properly completed Form 2 petition satisfies the requirements of this Rule.

(e) Original Required: Notwithstanding Rule 23(b), only the signed original of each petition is required to be filed.

RULE 35. ENTRY ON DOCKET

Upon receipt of the petition by the Clerk, the case will be entered upon the docket and assigned a number, and the parties will be notified thereof by the Clerk. The docket num- ber shall be placed by the parties on all papers thereafter filed in the case, and shall be referred to in all correspond- ence with the Court.

RULE 36. ANSWER

(a) Time To Answer or Move: The Commissioner shall have 60 days from the date of service of the petition within which to file an answer, or 45 days from that date within which to move with respect to the petition. With re- spect to an amended petition or amendments to the petition, the Commissioner shall have like periods from the date of service of those papers within which to answer or move in re- sponse thereto, except as the Court may otherwise direct.

(b) Form and Content: The answer shall be drawn so that it will advise the petitioner and the Court fully of the nature of the defense. It shall contain a specific admission or denial of each material allegation in the petition; however, if the Commissioner shall be without knowledge or information sufficient to form a belief as to the truth of an allegation, then the Commissioner shall so state, and such statement shall have the effect of a denial. If the Commissioner intends to qualify or to deny only a part of an allegation, then the Commissioner shall specify so much of it as is true and shall qualify or deny only the remainder. In addition, the answer shall contain a clear and concise statement of every ground, together with the facts in support thereof on which the Com- missioner relies and has the burden of proof. Paragraphs of the answer shall be designated to correspond to those of the petition to which they relate.

(c) Effect of Answer: Every material allegation set out in the petition and not expressly admitted or denied in the answer shall be deemed to be admitted.

(d) Declaratory Judgment, Disclosure, and Adminis- trative Costs Actions: For the requirements applicable to the answer in declaratory judgment actions, in disclosure ac- tions, and in administrative costs actions, see Rules 213(a), 223(a), and 272(a), respectively.

RULE 37. REPLY

29

(a) Time To Reply or Move: The petitioner shall have 45 days from the date of service of the answer within which to file a reply, or 30 days from that date within which to move with respect to the answer. With respect to an amend- ed answer or amendments to the answer the petitioner shall have like periods from the date of service of those papers within which to reply or move in response thereto, except as the Court may otherwise direct.

(b) Form and Content: In response to each material allegation in the answer and the facts in support thereof on which the Commissioner has the burden of proof, the reply shall contain a specific admission or denial; however, if the petitioner shall be without knowledge or information suffi- cient to form a belief as to the truth of an allegation, then   the petitioner shall so state, and such statement shall have   the effect of a denial. In addition, the reply shall contain a clear and concise statement of every ground, together with   the facts in support thereof, on which the petitioner relies af- firmatively or in avoidance of any matter in the answer on which the Commissioner has the burden of proof. In other re- spects the requirements of pleading applicable to the answer provided in Rule 36(b) shall apply to the reply. The para- graphs of the reply shall be designated to correspond to those of the answer to which they relate.

[1](c) Effect of Reply or Failure Thereof: Where a reply is filed, every affirmative allegation set out in the an- swer and not expressly admitted or denied in the reply shall be deemed to be admitted. Where a reply is not filed, the af- firmative allegations in the answer will be deemed denied unless the Commissioner, within 45 days after expiration of the time for filing the reply, files a motion that specified alle- gations in the answer be deemed admitted. That motion may be granted unless the required reply is filed within the time directed by the Court.

(d) New Material: Any new material contained in the reply shall be deemed to be denied.

(e) Declaratory Judgment, Disclosure, and Adminis- trative Costs Actions: For the requirements applicable to the reply in declaratory judgment actions and in disclosure actions, see Rules 213(b) and 223(b), respectively. See Rule 272(b) with respect to replies in actions for administrative costs.

RULE 38. JOINDER OF ISSUE

A case shall be deemed at issue upon the filing of the an- swer, unless a reply is required under Rule 37, in which event it shall be deemed at issue upon the filing of a reply   or the entry of an order disposing of a motion under Rule 37(c) or the expiration of the period specified in Rule 37(c) in case the Commissioner fails to move. With respect to declara- tory judgment actions, disclosure actions, partnership ac- tions, administrative costs actions, and actions for deter- mination of relief from joint and several liability on a joint return, see Rules 214, 224, 244, 273, and 324, respectively.

RULE 39. PLEADING SPECIAL MATTERS

A party shall set forth in the party's pleading any matter constituting an avoidance or affirmative defense, including res judicata, collateral estoppel, estoppel, waiver, duress, fraud, and the statute of limitations. A mere denial in a responsive pleading will not be sufficient to raise any such issue.

RULE 40. DEFENSES AND OBJECTIONS MADE BY PLEADING OR MOTION

Every defense, in law or fact, to a claim for relief in any pleading shall be asserted in the responsive pleading thereto if one is required, except that the following defenses may, at the option of the pleader, be made by motion: (a) Lack of jurisdiction, and (b) failure to state a claim upon which relief can be granted. If a pleading sets forth a claim for relief to which the adverse party is not required to file a responsive pleading, then such party may assert at the trial any defense in law or fact to that claim for relief. If, on a motion assert- ing failure to state a claim on which relief can be granted, matters outside the pleading are to be presented, then the motion shall be treated as one for summary judgment and disposed of as provided in Rule 121, and the parties shall be given an opportunity to present all material made pertinent to a motion under Rule 121.

RULE 41. AMENDED AND SUPPLEMENTAL PLEADINGS

(a) Amendments: A party may amend a pleading once as a matter of course at any time before a responsive pleading is served. If the pleading is one to which no responsive pleading is permitted and the case has not been placed on a trial calendar, then a party may so amend it at any time within 30 days after it is served. Otherwise a party may amend a pleading only by leave of Court or by written con- sent of the adverse party, and leave shall be given freely when justice so requires. No amendment shall be allowed after expiration of the time for filing the petition, however, which would involve conferring jurisdiction on the Court over a matter which otherwise would not come within its jurisdic- tion under the petition as then on file. A motion for leave to amend a pleading shall state the reasons for the amendment and shall be accompanied by the proposed amendment. The amendment to the pleading shall not be incorporated into the motion but rather shall be separately set forth and consistent with the requirements of Rule 23 regarding form and style of papers filed with the Court. See Rules 36(a) and 37(a) for time for responding to amended pleadings.

(b) Amendments To Conform to the Evidence: (1) *Issues Tried by Consent:* When issues not raised by the pleadings are tried by express or implied consent of the parties, they shall be treated in all respects as if they had been raised in the pleadings. The Court, upon motion of any party at any time, may allow such amendment of the pleadings as may be necessary to cause them to conform to the evidence and to raise these issues, but failure to amend does not affect the result of the trial of these issues.

(2) *Other Evidence:* If evidence is objected to at the trial on the ground that it is not within the issues raised by the pleadings, then the Court may receive the evidence and at any time allow the pleadings to be amended to con- form to the proof, and shall do so freely when justice so re- quires and the objecting party fails to satisfy the Court that the admission of such evidence would prejudice such party in maintaining such party's position on the merits.

(3) *Filing:* The amendment or amended pleadings per- mitted under this paragraph (b) shall be filed with the Court at the trial or shall be filed with the Clerk at Wash- ington, D.C., within such time as the Court may fix.

(c) Supplemental Pleadings: Upon motion of a party, the Court may, upon such terms as are just, permit a party to file a supplemental pleading setting forth transactions or occurrences or events which have happened since the date of the pleading sought to be supplemented. Permission may be granted even though the original pleading is defective in its statements of a claim for relief or defense. If the Court deems it advisable that the adverse party plead to the supplemental pleading, then it shall so direct, specifying the time therefor.

(d) Relation Back of Amendments: When an amend- ment of a pleading is permitted, it shall relate back to the time of filing of that pleading, unless the Court shall order otherwise either on motion of a party or on its own initiative.

TITLE V MOTIONS

RULE 50. GENERAL REQUIREMENTS

(a) Form and Content of Motion: An application to the Court for an order shall be by motion in writing, which shall state with particularity the grounds therefor and shall set forth the relief or order sought. The motion shall show that prior notice thereof has been given to each other party or counsel for each other party and shall state whether there is any objection to the motion. If a motion does not include such a statement, the Court will assume that there is an ob- jection to the motion. Unless the Court directs otherwise, mo- tions made during a hearing or trial need not be in writing. The rules applicable to captions, signing, and other matters of form and style of pleadings apply to all written motions. See Rules 23, 32, and 33(a). The effect of a signature on a motion shall be as set forth in Rule 33(b).

(b) Disposition of Motions: A motion may be disposed of in one or more of the following ways, in the discretion of the Court:

[1](1) The Court may take action after directing that a written response be filed. In that event, the opposing party shall file such response within such period as the Court may direct. Written response to a motion shall conform to the same requirements of form and style as apply to motions.

[2](2) The Court may take action after directing a hear- ing, which may be held in Washington, D.C. The Court may, on its own motion or upon the written request of any party to the motion, direct that the hearing be held at some other location which serves the convenience of the parties and the Court.

(3) The Court may take such action as the Court in its discretion deems appropriate, on such prior notice, if any, which the Court may consider reasonable. The action of the Court may be taken with or without written response, hearing, or attendance of a party to the motion at the hearing.

(c) Attendance at Hearings: If a motion is noticed for hearing, then a party to the motion may, prior to or at the time for such hearing, submit a written statement of such party's position together with any supporting documents. Such statement may be submitted in lieu of or in addition to attendance at the hearing.

(d) Defects in Pleading: Where the motion or order is directed to defects in a pleading, prompt filing of a proper pleading correcting the defects may obviate the necessity of a hearing thereon.

(e) Postponement of Trial: The filing of a motion shall not constitute cause for postponement of a trial. With respect to motions for continuance, see Rule 133.

[1]**(f) Effect of Orders:** Orders shall not be treated as precedent, except as may be relevant for purposes of estab- lishing the law of the case, res judicata, collateral estoppel, or other similar doctrine.

RULE 51. MOTION FOR MORE DEFINITE STATEMENT

(a) General: If a pleading to which a responsive plead- ing is permitted or required is so vague or ambiguous that a party cannot reasonably be required to frame a responsive pleading, then the party may move for a more definite statement before interposing a responsive pleading. The motion shall point out the defects complained of and the details desired. See Rules 70 and 90 for procedures available to narrow the issues or to elicit further information as to the facts involved or the positions of the parties.

(b) Penalty for Failure of Response: The Court may strike the pleading to which the motion is directed or may make such other order as it deems just, if the required response is not made within such period as the Court may direct.

RULE 52. MOTION TO STRIKE

Upon motion made by a party before responding to a pleading or, if no responsive pleading is permitted by these Rules, upon motion made by a party within 30 days after the service of the pleading, or upon the Court's own initiative at any time, the Court may order stricken from any pleading any insufficient claim or defense or any redundant, immate- rial, impertinent, frivolous, or scandalous matter. In like manner and procedure, the Court may order stricken any such objectionable matter from briefs, documents, or any other papers or responses filed with the Court.

RULE 53. MOTION TO DISMISS

A case may be dismissed for cause upon motion of a party or upon the Court's initiative.

RULE 54. TIMELY FILING AND JOINDER OF MOTIONS

(a) Timely Filing: Unless otherwise permitted by the Court, motions must be made timely.

(b) Joinder of Motions: Unless otherwise permitted by the Court, motions shall be separately stated and not joined together, except that motions may be joined in the fol- lowing instances: (1) Motions under Rules 51 and 52 directed to the same pleading or other paper; and (2) motions under Rule 56 for the review of a jeopardy assessment and for the review of a jeopardy levy, but only if the assessment and the levy are the subject of the same written statement required by Code section 7429(a)(1).

RULE 55. MOTION TO RESTRAIN ASSESSMENT OR COLLECTION OR TO ORDER REFUND OF AMOUNT COLLECTED

A motion to restrain assessment or collection or to order refund of any amount collected may be filed with the Court only where a timely petition has been filed with the Court. See Code secs. 6015(e)(1)(B)(ii), 6213(a), 6225(b), 6246(b), 6330(e), 7436(d). For the rules applicable to captions, signing, and other matters of form and style of motions, see Rule 50(a).

RULE 56. MOTION FOR REVIEW OF JEOPARDY ASSESSMENT OR JEOPARDY LEVY

(a) Commencement of Review: (1) *How Review Is Commenced:* Review of a jeopardy assessment or a jeopardy levy under Code section 7429(b) shall be commenced by filing a motion with the Court. The petitioner shall place on the motion the same docket number as that of a then-pending action under Code section 6213(a) which provides the jurisdictional nexus for review required by Code section 7429(b)(2)(B). The motion shall be styled "Motion for Review of Jeopardy Assessment" or "Motion for Review of Jeopardy Levy", as may be appropriate. As to joinder of such motions, see Rule 54(b).

(2) *When Review Is Commenced:* The motion under subparagraph (1) shall be filed within the time provided by Code section 7429(b)(1).

(b) Service of Motion: A motion filed with the Court pursuant to this Rule shall be served by the petitioner on counsel for the Commissioner (as specified in Rule 21(b)(1)) in such manner as may reasonably be expected to reach the Commissioner's counsel not later than the day on which the motion is received by the Court.

(c) Content of Motion: A motion filed pursuant to this Rule shall contain the following:

(1) A statement whether the petitioner contends that:

(A) The making of the assessment in respect of which the motion is filed was not reasonable under the circumstances;

(B) the amount so assessed or demanded is not appropriate under the circumstances; or

(C) the levy in respect of which the motion is filed was not reasonable under the circumstances.

(2) As to each contention in paragraph (c)(1) of this Rule:

(A) Clear and concise assignments of each and every error which the petitioner alleges to have been com- mitted by the Commissioner; and

(B) clear and concise lettered statements of the facts on which the petitioner bases the assignments of error.

(3) As to the contention in paragraph (c)(1)(B) of this Rule, a statement of the amount, if any, that would be appropriate under the circumstances.

(4) A statement whether the petitioner requests an evi-

dentiary or other hearing on the motion, and if so, the reasons why. For the place of hearing, see paragraph (e) of this Rule.

(5) A list identifying by caption and number all other dockets in which the motion could have been filed if more than one then-pending action for the redetermination of a deficiency under Code section 6213(a) provides the jurisdictional nexus for review required by Code section 7429(b)(2)(B).

(6) A copy of:

(A) The written statement required to be furnished to the petitioner under Code section 7429(a)(1), together with any notice or other document regarding the jeop- ardy assessment or jeopardy levy that may have been served on the petitioner by the Commissioner and in re- spect of which the motion is filed;

(B) the request for administrative review made by the petitioner under Code section 7429(a)(2); and

(C) the determination made by the Commissioner under Code section 7429(a)(3).

(7) A certificate showing service of the motion in accordance with paragraph (b) of this Rule.

(d) Response by Commissioner: (1) *Content:* The Commissioner shall file a written response to a motion filed pursuant to this Rule. The response shall contain the following:

(A) A specific admission or denial of each allegation in the motion, arranged in paragraphs that are des- ignated to correspond to those of the motion to which they relate.

(B) A clear and concise statement of every ground, together with the facts in support thereof, on which the Commissioner relies.

(C) A statement whether the Commissioner requests a hearing on the motion, and if so, the reasons why.

(D) A copy of:

(i) The written notification to the Court required by Code section 6861(c); and

(ii) any item required for consideration of the basis of the petitioner's motion, if that item has not been attached to the petitioner's motion.

(E) A certificate showing service of the response in accordance with subparagraph (2) of this paragraph.

(2) *Time for and Service of Response:* The response required by paragraph (d)(1) of this Rule shall be received by the Court not later than 10 days after the date on which the petitioner's motion is received by the Court. Said re- sponse shall be served by the Commissioner in such man- ner as may reasonably be expected to reach the petitioner or the petitioner's counsel (as specified in Rule 21(b)(2)) not later than the day on which the response is received by the Court.

(e) Place of Hearing: If required, a hearing on the mo- tion filed pursuant to this Rule will ordinarily be held at the place of trial previously requested in accordance with para- graph (a) of Rule 140 unless otherwise ordered by the Court.

RULE 57. MOTION FOR REVIEW OF PROPOSED SALE OF SEIZED PROPERTY

(a) Commencement of Review: (1) *How Review Is Commenced:* Review of the Commissioner's determination under Code section 6863(b)(3)(B) that seized property may be sold shall be commenced by filing a motion with the Court. The movant shall place on the motion the same docket num- ber as that of the then-pending action under Code section 6213(a) in respect of which the sale of seized property is stayed by virtue of Code section 6863(b)(3)(A)(iii). If filed by the petitioner, the motion shall be styled ''Motion to Stay Proposed Sale of Seized Property—Sec. 6863(b)(3)(C)''. If filed by the Commissioner, the motion shall be styled ''Motion to Authorize Proposed Sale of Seized Property—Sec. 6863(b)(3)(C)''.

(2) *When Review Is Commenced:* (A) *Proposed Sale Not Scheduled:* If a date for a proposed sale has not been scheduled, then the Commissioner may file the motion under subparagraph (1) at any time.

(B) *Proposed Sale Scheduled:* (i) *General:* If a date for a proposed sale has been scheduled, then the movant shall file the motion under subparagraph (1) not less than 15 days before the date of the proposed sale

and not more than 20 days after receipt of the notice of sale prescribed by Code section 6335(b).

(ii) *Motion Not Filed Within Prescribed Period:* If the motion under subparagraph (1) is filed less than 15 days before the date of the proposed sale or more than 20 days after receipt of the notice of sale pre- scribed by Code section 6335(b), then an additional statement shall be included in the motion as provided by paragraph (c)(3) of this Rule. A motion not filed within the period prescribed by subparagraph (2)(B)(i) shall be considered dilatory unless the movant shows that there was good reason for not filing the motion within that period. As to the effect of the motion's being dilatory, see paragraph (g)(4) of this Rule.

(b) Service of Motion: (1) *By the Petitioner:* A mo- tion filed with the Court pursuant to this Rule shall be served by the petitioner on counsel for the Commissioner (as specified in Rule 21(b)(1)) in such manner as may reasonably be expected to reach the Commissioner's counsel not later than the day on which the motion is received by the Court.

(2) *By the Commissioner:* A motion filed with the Court pursuant to this Rule shall be served by the Com- missioner on the petitioner or on the petitioner's counsel (as specified in Rule 21(b)(2)) in such manner as may rea- sonably be

expected to reach the petitioner or the peti- tioner's counsel not later than the day on which the motion is received by the Court.

(c) Content of Motion: A motion filed pursuant to this Rule shall contain the following:

(1) The time and place of the proposed sale.

(2) A description of the property proposed to be sold, together with a copy of the notice of seizure prescribed by Code section 6335(a) and the notice of sale prescribed by Code section 6335(b).

(3) If the motion is filed less than 15 days before the date of the proposed sale or more than 20 days after re- ceipt of the notice of sale prescribed by Code section 6335(b), as the case may be, a statement of the reasons why review was not commenced within the prescribed pe- riod.

(4) A statement that the petitioner does not consent to the proposed sale.

(5) A statement whether the property proposed to be sold—

(A) is or is not likely to perish;

(B) is or is not likely to become greatly reduced in price or value by keeping; and

(C) is or is not likely to be greatly expensive to conserve or maintain.

[1](6) The movant's basis for each statement in subparagraph (5) that the movant expressed in the affirmative, together with any appraisal, affidavit or declaration, valu- ation report, or other document relied on by the movant to support each statement.

(7) A statement whether the movant requests an evidentiary or other hearing on the motion, and if so, the reasons why. For the place of hearing, see paragraph (f) of this Rule.

(8) A certificate showing service of the motion in accordance with paragraph (b) of this Rule.

(d) Response to Motion: (1) *Content:* The petitioner or the Commissioner, as the case may be, shall file a written response to a motion filed pursuant to this Rule. The re- sponse shall contain the following:

(A) A specific admission or denial of each allegation in the motion arranged in paragraphs that are des- ignated to correspond to those of the motion to which they relate.

(B) A clear and concise statement of every ground, together with the facts in support thereof, on which the responding party relies.

(C) A statement whether the responding party re- quests a hearing on the motion, and if so, the reasons why.

(D) A copy of:

[2](i) Any appraisal, affidavit or declaration, valu- ation report, or other document relied on by the re- sponding

38

party; and

(ii) any item required for consideration of the basis of the movant's motion, if that item has not been attached to the movant's motion.

A certificate showing service of the response in accordance with subparagraph (2) of this paragraph.

(2) *Time for and Service of Response:* The response required by paragraph (d)(1) of this Rule shall be received by the Court not later than 10 days after the date on which the movant's motion is received by the Court. This re- sponse shall be served in such manner as may reasonably be expected to reach the movant or the movant's counsel (as specified in Rule 21(b)(1) or Rule 21(b)(2), as the case may be) not later than the day on which the response is received by the Court.

(e) **Effect of Signature:** The provisions of Rule 33(b), relating to the effect of the signature of counsel or a party, shall apply to a motion filed pursuant to this Rule and to the response required by paragraph (d) of this Rule.

(f) **Place of Hearing:** If required, a hearing on a mo- tion filed pursuant to this Rule will ordinarily be held at the place of trial previously requested in accordance with para- graph (a) of Rule 140 unless otherwise ordered by the Court. For the manner in which the Court may dispose of such a motion, see paragraph (g)(3) of this Rule.

(g) **Disposition of Motion:** (1) *General:* A motion filed pursuant to this Rule may be disposed of in one or more of the following ways, in the discretion of the Court:

(A) The Court may:

(i) Authorize, or decline to stay, the proposed sale; or

(ii) stay the proposed sale temporarily until the Court has had an adequate opportunity to consider the motion.

(B) The Court may stay the proposed sale until a specified date or event, or for a specified period, or until further application is made for a sale, or any combina- tion of the foregoing.

(C) The Court may stay the proposed sale until speci- fied undertakings or safeguards are effectuated.

(D) The Court may provide such other temporary, ex- tended, or permanent relief as may be appropriate under the circumstances.

[1](2) *Evidence:* In disposing of a motion filed pursuant to this Rule, the Court may consider such appraisals, affi- davits or declarations, valuation reports, and other evidence as may be appropriate, giving due regard to the necessity of acting on the motion within a brief period of time.

(3) *Disposition on Motion Papers or Otherwise:* The Court may dispose of a motion filed pursuant to this Rule on the motion papers, or after an evidentiary hearing or oral

argument, or may require legal memoranda, or any combination of the foregoing that the Court deems appropriate. For the place of hearing, see paragraph (f) of this Rule.

(4) *Dilatory Motions:* The fact that a motion filed pursuant to this Rule is dilatory within the meaning of paragraph (a)(2)(B)(ii) of this Rule shall be considered by the Court in disposing of the motion.

RULE 58. MISCELLANEOUS

For reference in the Rules to other motions, see Rules 25(c) (extension of time), 40 (defenses made by motion), 41 (amendment of pleadings), 63 (substitution of parties), 71(c) (answers to interrogatories), 81(b) (depositions), 90(e) (requests for admission), 91(f) (stipulations), 121(a) (summary judgment), 123(c) (setting aside default or dismissal), 133 (continuances), 140(c) (place of trial), 141 (consolidation and separation), 151(c) (delinquent briefs), 157 (retention of official case file in estate tax case involving election under Code section 6166), 161 (reconsideration), 162 (vacating or revising decision), 231 (reasonable litigation and administrative costs), 260 (enforcement of overpayment determination), 261 (redetermination of interest on deficiency), and 262 (modification of decision in estate tax case involving election under Code section 6166).

TITLE VI PARTIES

RULE 60. PROPER PARTIES; CAPACITY

(a) **Petitioner:** (1) *Deficiency or Liability Action:* A case shall be brought by and in the name of the person against whom the Commissioner determined the deficiency (in the case of a notice of deficiency) or liability (in the case of a notice of liability), or by and with the full descriptive name of the fiduciary entitled to institute a case on behalf   of such person. See Rule 23(a)(1). A case timely brought shall not be dismissed on the ground that it is not properly brought on behalf of a party until a reasonable time has been allowed after objection for ratification by such party of the bringing of the case; and such ratification shall have the   same effect as if the case had been properly brought by such party. Where the deficiency or liability is determined against more than one person in the notice by the Commissioner, only such of those persons who shall duly act to bring a case shall be deemed a party or parties.

(2) *Other Actions:* For the person who may bring a case as a petitioner in a declaratory judgment action, see Rules 210(b)(13), 211, and 216. For the person who may bring a case as a petitioner in a disclosure action, see   Rules 220(b)(5), 221, and 225. For the person who may bring a case as a petitioner in a partnership action, see Rules 240(c)(1)(B), 240(c)(2)(B), 241, 245, 300(c)(1)(B), 300(c)(2)(B), and 301.

For the person who may bring a case as a petitioner in an action for redetermination of employ- ment status, see Rule 290(b)(2).

(b) Respondent: The Commissioner shall be named the respondent.

(c) Capacity: The capacity of an individual, other than one acting in a fiduciary or other representative capacity, to engage in litigation in the Court shall be determined by the law of the individual's domicile. The capacity of a corporation to engage in such litigation shall be determined by the law under which it was organized. The capacity of a fiduciary or other representative to litigate in the Court shall be deter- mined in accordance with the law of the jurisdiction from which such person's authority is derived.

(d) Infants or Incompetent Persons: Whenever an infant or incompetent person has a representative, such as a general guardian, committee, conservator, or other like fidu- ciary, the representative may bring a case or defend in the Court on behalf of the infant or incompetent person. An in- fant or incompetent person who does not have a duly ap- pointed representative may act by a next friend or by a guardian ad litem. Where a party attempts to represent him- self or herself and, in the opinion of the Court there is a seri- ous question as to such party's competence to do so, the Court, if it deems justice so requires, may continue the case until appropriate steps have been taken to obtain an adju- dication of the question by a court having jurisdiction to do so, or may take such other action as it deems proper.

RULE 61. PERMISSIVE JOINDER OF PARTIES

(a) Permissive Joinder: No person, to whom a notice of deficiency or notice of liability has been issued, may join with any other such person in filing a petition in the Court, except as may be permitted by Rule 34(a)(1). With respect to the joinder of parties in declaratory judgment actions, see Rule 215; in disclosure actions, see Rule 226; and in partner- ship actions, see Rules 241(h) and 301(f).

(b) Severance or Other Orders: The Court may make such orders as will prevent a party from being embarrassed, delayed, or put to expense by the inclusion of a party, or may order separate trials or make other orders to prevent delay or prejudice; or may limit the trial to the claims of one or more parties, either dropping other parties from the case on such terms as are just or holding in abeyance the pro- ceedings with respect to them. Any claim by or against a party may be severed and proceeded with separately. See also Rule 141(b).

RULE 62. MISJOINDER OF PARTIES

Misjoinder of parties is not ground for dismissal of a case. The Court may order a severance on such terms as are just. See Rule 61(b).

RULE 63. SUBSTITUTION OF PARTIES; CHANGE OR CORRECTION IN NAME

(a) Death: If a petitioner dies, the Court, on motion of a party or the decedent's successor or representative or on its own initiative, may order substitution of the proper parties.

(b) Incompetency: If a party becomes incompetent, the Court, on motion of a party or the incompetent's representative or on its own initiative, may order the representative to proceed with the case.

(c) Successor Fiduciaries or Representatives: On motion made where a fiduciary or representative is changed, the Court may order substitution of the proper successors.

(d) Other Cause: The Court, on motion of a party or on its own initiative, may order the substitution of proper parties for other cause.

(e) Change or Correction in Name: On motion of a party or on its own initiative, the Court may order a change of or correction in the name or title of a party.

TITLE VII DISCOVERY

RULE 70. GENERAL PROVISIONS

(a) General: [1](1) *Methods and Limitations of Discovery:* In conformity with these Rules, a party may obtain discovery by written interrogatories (Rule 71), by production of documents, electronically stored information, or things (Rules 72 and 73), by depositions upon consent of the parties (Rule 74(b)), or by depositions without consent of the parties in certain cases (Rule 74(c)). However, the Court expects the parties to attempt to attain the objectives of discovery through informal consultation or communication before uti- lizing the discovery procedures provided in these Rules. Dis- covery is not available under these Rules through depositions except to the limited extent provided in Rule 74. See Rules 91(a) and 100 regarding relationship of discovery to stipula- tions.

[2](2) *Time for Discovery:* Discovery shall not be commenced, without leave of Court, before the expiration of 30 days after joinder of issue (see Rule 38). Discovery shall be completed and any motion to compel or any other motion with respect to such discovery shall be filed, unless otherwise authorized by the Court, no later than 45 days prior to the date set for call of the case from a trial calendar. Discovery by a deposition under Rule 74(c) may not be commenced before a notice of trial has been issued or the case has been assigned to a Judge or Special Trial Judge and

42

any motion to compel or any other motion with respect to such discovery shall be filed within the time provided by the preceding sentence. Discovery of matters which are rel- evant only to the issue of a party's entitlement to reason- able litigation or administrative costs shall not be com- menced, without leave of Court, before a motion for reason- able litigation or administrative costs has been noticed for a hearing, and discovery shall be completed and any mo- tion to compel or any other motion with respect to suchdiscovery shall be filed, unless otherwise authorized by the Court, no later than 45 days prior to the date set for hear- ing.

(3) *Cases Consolidated for Trial:* With respect to a common matter in cases consolidated for trial, discovery may be had by any party to such a case to the extent pro- vided by these Rules, and, for that purpose, the reference to a ''party'' in this Title VII, in Title VIII, or in Title X, shall mean any party to any of the consolidated cases in- volving such common matter.

[1](b) **Scope of Discovery:** The information or response sought through discovery may concern any matter not privi- leged and which is relevant to the subject matter involved in the pending case. It is not ground for objection that the infor- mation or response sought will be inadmissible at the trial, if that information or response appears reasonably calculated to lead to discovery of admissible evidence, regardless of the burden of proof involved. If the information or response sought is otherwise proper, it is not objectionable merely be- cause the information or response involves an opinion or con- tention that relates to fact or to the application of law to fact. But the Court may order that the information or response sought need not be furnished or made until some designated time or a particular stage has been reached in the case or until a specified step has been taken by a party.

[2](c) **Limitations on Discovery:** (1) *General:* The frequency or extent of use of the discovery methods set forth in paragraph (a) shall be limited by the Court if it deter- mines that: (A) The discovery sought is unreasonably cumu- lative or duplicative, or is obtainable from some other source that is more convenient, less burdensome, or less expensive;
(B) the party seeking discovery has had ample opportunity by discovery in the action to obtain the information sought; or (C) the discovery is unduly burdensome or expensive, taking into account the needs of the case, the amount in controversy, limitations on the parties' resources, and the importance of the issues at stake in the litigation. The Court may act upon its own initiative after reasonable notice or pursuant to a motion under Rule 103.

(2) *Electronically Stored Information:* A party need not provide discovery of electronically stored information from sources that the party identifies as not reasonably accessible

because of undue burden or cost. On motion to compel discovery or for a protective order, the party from whom discovery is sought must show that the information is not reasonably accessible because of undue burden or cost. If that showing is made, the Court may nonetheless order discovery from such sources if the requesting party shows good cause, considering the limitations of Rule 70(c)(1). The Court may specify conditions for the dis- covery.

(3)   Documents and Tangible Things:

(A)   A party generally may not discover documents and tangible things that are prepared in anticipation of litigation or for trial by or for another party or its representative (including the other party's attorney, consultant, surety, indemnitor, insurer, or agent), unless, subject to Rule 70(c)(4),

(i)   they are otherwise discoverable under Rule 70(b); and

(ii)   the party shows that it has substantial need for the materials to prepare its case and cannot, without undue hardship, obtain their substantial equivalent by other means.

(B)   If the Court orders discovery of those materials, it must protect against disclosure of mental impressions, conclusions, opinions, or legal theories of a party's counsel or other representative concerning the litigation.

(4)   Experts:

(A)   Rule 70(c)(3) protects drafts of any expert witness report required under Rule 143(g), regardless of the form in which the draft is recorded.

(B)   Rule 70(c)(3) protects communications between a party's counsel and any witness required to provide a report under Rule 143(g), regardless of the form of the communications, except to the extent the communications:

(i)   relate to compensation for the expert's study or testimony;

(ii)   identify facts or data that the party's counsel provided and that the expert considered in forming the opinions to be expressed; or

(iii)   identify assumptions that the party's counsel provided and that the expert relied on in forming the opinions to be expressed.

(C)   A party generally may not, by interrogatories or depositions, discover facts known or opinions held by an expert who has been retained or specially employed by another party in anticipation of litigation or to prepare for trial and who is not expected to be called as a witness at trial, except on a showing of exceptional circumstances under which it is impracticable for the party to obtain facts or opinions on the same subject by other means.

[1](d) Party's Statements: Upon request to the other party and without any showing except the assertion in writing that the requester lacks and has no convenient means of obtaining a copy of a statement made by the requester, a party shall be entitled to obtain a copy of any such statement which has a bearing on the subject matter of the case and is in the possession or control of another party to the case.

[2](e) Use In Case: The answers to interrogatories, things produced in response to a request, or other information or responses obtained under Rules 71, 72, 73, and 74 may be used at trial or in any proceeding in the case prior or subsequent to trial to the extent permitted by the rules of evidence. Such answers or information or responses will not be considered as evidence until offered and received as evidence. No objections to interrogatories or the answers thereto, or to a request to produce or the response thereto, will be considered unless made within the time prescribed, except that the objection that an interrogatory or answer would be inadmissible at trial is preserved even though not made prior to trial.

[1](f) Signing of Discovery Requests, Responses, and Objections: (1) Every request for discovery or response or objection thereto made by a party represented by counsel shall be signed by at least one counsel of record. A party who is not represented by counsel shall sign the request, response, or objection. The signature shall conform to the requirements of Rule 23(a)(3). The signature of counsel or a party constitutes a certification that the signer has read the request, response, or objection, and that to the best of the signer's knowledge, information, and belief formed after a reasonable inquiry, it is: (A) Consistent with these Rules and warranted by existing law or a good faith argument for the extension, modification, or reversal of existing law, (B) not interposed for any improper purpose, such as to harass or to cause unnecessary delay or needless increase in the cost of litigation, and (C) not unreasonable or unduly burdensome or expensive, given the needs of the case, the discovery already had in the case, the amount in controversy, and the importance of the issues at stake in the litigation. If a request, response, or objection is not signed, then it shall be stricken, unless it is signed promptly after the omission is called to the attention of the party making the request, response, or objection, and a party shall not be obligated to take any action with respect to it until it is signed.

(2) If a certification is made in violation of this Rule, then the Court upon motion or upon its own initiative, may impose upon the person who made the certification, the party on whose behalf the request, response, or objection is made, or

both, an appropriate sanction, which may include an order to pay the amount of the reasonable expenses incurred because of the violation, including reason- able counsel's fees.

[2](g) **Other Applicable Rules:** For Rules concerned with the frequency and timing of discovery in relation to other procedures, supplementation of answers, protective orders, effect of evasive or incomplete answers or responses, and sanctions and enforcement action, see Title X.

RULE 71. INTERROGATORIES

[1](a) **Availability:** Unless otherwise stipulated or ordered by the Court, a party may serve upon any other party no more than 25 written interrogatories, including all discrete subparts but excluding interrogatories described in paragraph (d) of this Rule, to be answered by the party served or, if the party served is a public or private corporation or a partnership or association or governmental agency, by an officer or agent who shall furnish such information as is available to the party. A motion for leave to serve additional interrogatories may be granted by the Court to the ex- tent consistent with Rule 70(c)(1).

(b) **Answers:** All answers shall be made in good faith and as completely as the answering party's information shall permit. However, the answering party is required to make reasonable inquiry and ascertain readily obtainable informa- tion. An answering party may not give lack of information or knowledge as an answer or as a reason for failure to answer, unless such party states that such party has made reason- able inquiry and that information known or readily obtain- able by such party is insufficient to enable such party to an- swer the substance of the interrogatory.

(c) **Procedure:** Each interrogatory shall be answered separately and fully under oath, unless it is objected to, in which event the reasons for the objection shall be stated in lieu of the answer. The answers are to be signed by the per- son making them and the objections shall be signed by the party or the party's counsel. The party on whom the interrog- atories have been served shall serve a copy of the answers, and objections if any, upon the propounding party within 30 days after service of the interrogatories. The Court may allow a shorter or longer time. The burden shall be on the party submitting the interrogatories to move for an order with respect to any objection or other failure to answer an interrogatory, and in that connection the moving party shall annex the interrogatories to the motion, with proof of service on the other party, together with the answers and objections, if any. Prior to a motion for such an order, neither the inter- rogatories nor the response shall be filed with the Court.

(d) **Experts:** (1) By means of written interrogatories in

conformity with this Rule, a party may require any other party: (A) To identify each person whom the other party ex- pects to call as an expert witness at the trial of the case, giv- ing the witness's name, address, vocation or occupation, and a statement of the witness's qualifications, and (B) to state the subject matter and the substance of the facts and opin- ions to which the expert is expected to testify, and give a summary of the grounds for each such opinion, or, in lieu of such statement to furnish a copy of a report of such expert presenting the foregoing information.

[1](2) For provisions regarding the submission and ex- change of expert witness reports, see Rule 143(g). That Rule shall not serve to extend the period of time under paragraph (c) of this Rule within which a party must an- swer any interrogatory directed at discovering: (A) The identity and qualifications of each person whom such party expects to call as an expert witness at the trial of the case and (B) the subject matter with respect to which the expert is expected to testify.

[2](e) **Option To Produce Business Records:** If the answer to an interrogatory may be derived or ascertained from the business records (including electronically stored in- formation) of the party upon whom the interrogatory has been served, or from an examination, audit, or inspection of such records, or from a compilation, abstract, or summary based thereon, and the burden of deriving or ascertaining the answer is substantially the same for the party serving the in- terrogatory as for the party served, it is sufficient answer to such interrogatory to specify the records from which the an- swer may be derived or ascertained and to afford to the party serving the interrogatory reasonable opportunity to examine, audit, or inspect such records and to make copies, compila- tions, abstracts, or summaries.

RULE 72. PRODUCTION OF DOCUMENTS, ELECTRONICALLY STORED INFORMATION, AND THINGS[1]

(a) Scope: Any party may, without leave of Court, serve on any other party a request to:

(1) Produce and permit the party making the request, or someone acting on such party's behalf, to inspect and copy, test, or sample any designated documents or elec- tronically stored information (including writings, drawings, graphs, charts, photographs, sound recordings, images, and other data compilations stored in any medium from which information can be obtained, either directly or translated, if necessary, by the responding party into a reasonably us- able form), or to inspect and copy, test, or sample any tan- gible thing, to the extent that any of the foregoing items are in the possession, custody, or control of the party on whom the request is served; or

47

(2)   Permit entry upon designated land or other prop- erty in the possession or control of the party upon whom   the request is served for the purpose of inspection and measuring, surveying, photographing, testing, or sampling the property or any designated object or operation thereon.

(b)   Procedure: (1) *Contents of the Request:* The re- quest shall set forth the items to be inspected, either by indi- vidual item or category, describe each item and category with reasonable particularity, and may specify the form or forms   in which electronically stored information is to be produced.   It shall specify a reasonable time, place, and manner of mak- ing the inspection and performing the related acts.

(2) *Responses and Objections:* The party upon whom the request is served shall serve a written response within 30 days after service of the request. The Court may allow a shorter or longer time. The response shall state, with re- spect to each item or category, that inspection and related activities will be permitted as requested, unless the re- quest is objected to in whole or in part, in which event the reasons for objection shall be stated. If objection is made to part of an item or category, then that part shall be spec- ified. The response may state an objection to a requested form for producing electronically stored information. If the responding party objects to a requested form—or if no form was specified in the request—the party shall state the form or forms it intends to use. To obtain a ruling on an objec- tion by the responding party, on a failure to respond, or on a failure to produce or permit inspection, the requesting party shall file an appropriate motion with the Court and shall annex thereto the request, with proof of service on   the other party, together with the response and objections   if any. Prior to a motion for such a ruling, neither the re- quest nor the response shall be filed with the Court.

(3) *Producing Documents or Electronically Stored Infor- mation:* Unless otherwise stipulated or ordered by the Court, these   procedures   apply   to   producing   documents   or electronically stored information: (A) A party shall produce documents as they are kept in the usual course of business or shall organize and label them to correspond to the cat- egories in the request; (B) If a request does not specify a form for producing electronically stored information, a party shall produce it in a form or forms in which it is or- dinarily maintained or in a reasonably usable form or forms; and (C) A party need not produce the same elec- tronically stored information in more than one form.

(c)   Foreign Petitioners: For production of records by foreign petitioners, see Code section 7456(b).

RULE 73. EXAMINATION BY TRANSFEREES [1]

(a)   General: Upon application to the Court and subject   to these Rules, a transferee of property of a taxpayer shall be entitled to examine before trial the books, papers, documents, correspondence, electronically stored information, and other evidence of the taxpayer or of a preceding transferee of the taxpayer's property, but only if the transferee making the application is a petitioner seeking redetermination of such transferee's liability in respect of the taxpayer's tax liability (including interest, additional amounts, and additions provided by law). Such books, papers, documents, correspondence, electronically stored information, and other evidence may be made available to the extent that the same shall be within the United States, will not result in undue hardship to the taxpayer or preceding transferee, and in the opinion of the Court are necessary in order to enable the transferee to ascertain the liability of the taxpayer or preceding transferee.

(b) Procedure: A petitioner desiring an examination permitted under paragraph (a) shall file an application with the Court, showing that such petitioner is entitled to such an examination, describing the documents, electronically stored information, and other materials sought to be examined, giving the names and addresses of the persons to produce the same, and stating a reasonable time and place where the examination is to be made. If the Court shall determine that the applicable requirements are satisfied, then it shall issue a subpoena, signed by a Judge, directed to the appropriate person and ordering the production at a designated time and place of the documents, electronically stored information, and other materials involved. If the person to whom the subpoena is directed shall object thereto or to the production involved, then such person shall file the objections and the reasons therefor in writing with the Court, and serve a copy thereof upon the applicant, within 10 days after service of the subpoena or on or before such earlier time as may be specified in the subpoena for compliance. To obtain a ruling on such objections, the applicant for the subpoena shall file an appropriate motion with the Court. In all respects not inconsistent with the provisions of this Rule, the provisions of Rule 72(b) shall apply where appropriate.

(c) Scope of Examination: The scope of the examination authorized under this Rule shall be as broad as is authorized under Rule 72(a), including, for example, the copying of such documents, electronically stored information, and materials.

RULE 74. DEPOSITIONS FOR DISCOVERY PURPOSES [1]

[2]**(a) General:** In conformity with this Rule, a party may obtain discovery by depositions with the consent of the parties under paragraph (b) and without the consent of the parties

under paragraph (c). Paragraph (d) describes additional uses for depositions of expert witnesses, and paragraphs (e) and (f) set forth general provisions governing the taking of all depositions for discovery purposes. An application for an order to take a deposition is required only with respect to depositions to perpetuate evidence. See Rules 80 through 84.

(b) Depositions Upon Consent of the Parties: (1) *When Deposition May Be Taken:* Upon consent of all the parties to a case, and within the time limits provided in Rule 70(a)(2), a deposition for discovery purposes may be taken of either a party, a nonparty witness, or an expert witness. Such consent shall be set forth in a stipulation filed in dupli- cate with the Court, which shall contain the information re- quired in Rule 81(d) and which otherwise shall be subject to the procedure provided in Rule 81(d).

(2) *Notice to Nonparty Witness or Expert Witness:* A notice of deposition shall be served on a nonparty witness or an expert witness. The notice shall state that the depo- sition is to be taken under Rule 74(b) and shall set forth the name of the party or parties seeking the deposition; the name and address of the person to be deposed; the time and place proposed for the deposition; the name of the offi- cer before whom the deposition is to be taken; a statement describing any books, papers, documents, electronically stored information, or tangible things to be produced at the deposition; and a statement of the issues in controversy to which the expected testimony of the witness, or the docu- ment, electronically stored information, or thing relates, and the reasons for deposing the witness. With respect to the deposition of an organization described in Rule 81(c), the notice shall also set forth the information requiredunder that Rule, and the organization shall make the des- ignation authorized by that Rule.

(3) *Objection by Nonparty Witness or Expert Witness:* Within 15 days after service of the notice of deposition, a nonparty witness or expert witness shall serve on the par- ties seeking the deposition any objections to the deposition. The burden shall be upon a party seeking the deposition to move for an order with respect to such objection or other failure of the nonparty witness or expert witness, and such party shall annex to any such motion the notice of deposi- tion with proof of service thereof, together with a copy of the response and objections, if any.

(c) Depositions Without Consent of the Parties: (1) *General:* (A) *When Depositions May Be Taken:* After a notice of trial has been issued or after a case has been assigned to a Judge or Special Trial Judge of the Court, and within the time for completion of discovery under Rule 70(a)(2), any party may take a deposition for discovery purposes of a party, a nonparty witness, or an expert witness in the cir- cumstances described in this paragraph.

(B) *Availability:* The taking of a deposition of a party, a nonparty witness, or an expert witness under this para- graph is an extraordinary method of discovery and may be used only where a party, a nonparty witness, or an expert witness can give testimony or possesses documents, elec- tronically stored information, or things which are discover- able within the meaning of Rule 70(b) and where such tes- timony, documents, electronically stored information, or things practicably cannot be obtained through informal consultation or communication (Rule 70(a)(1)), interrog- atories (Rule 71), a request for production of documents, electronically stored information, or things (Rule 72), or by a deposition taken with consent of the parties (Rule 74(b)). If such requirements are satisfied, then a deposition of a witness may be taken under this paragraph, for example, where a party is a member of a partnership and an issue in the case involves an adjustment with respect to such partnership, or a party is a shareholder of an S corporation (as described in Code section 1361(a)), and an issue in the case involves an adjustment with respect to such S cor- poration. See Title XXIV, relating to partnership actions, brought under provisions first enacted by the Tax Equity and Fiscal Responsibility Act of 1982.

(2) *Nonparty Witnesses:* A party may take the deposi- tion of a nonparty witness without leave of court and with- out the consent of all the parties as follows:

(A) *Notice:* A party desiring to take a deposition under this subparagraph shall give notice in writing to every other party to the case and to the nonparty wit- ness to be deposed. The notice shall state that the deposition is to be taken under Rule 74(c)(2) and shall set forth the name of the party seeking the deposition; the name and address of the person to be deposed; the time and place proposed for the deposition; the officer before whom the deposition is to be taken; a statement describ- ing any books, papers, documents, electronically stored information, or tangible things to be produced at the deposition; and a statement of the issues in controversy to which the expected testimony of the witness, or the document, electronically stored information, or thing re- lates, and the reasons for deposing the witness. With re- spect to the deposition of an organization described in Rule 81(c), the notice shall also set forth the information required under that Rule, and the organization shall make the designation authorized by that Rule.

(B) *Objections:* Within 15 days after service of the notice of deposition, a party or a nonparty witness shall serve on the party seeking the deposition any objections to the deposition. The burden shall be upon the party seeking the deposition to move for an order with respect to any such

51

objections or any failure of the nonparty wit- ness, and such party shall annex to any such motion the notice of deposition with proof of service thereof, together with a copy of any responses and objections. Prior to a motion for such an order, neither the notice nor the re- sponses shall be filed with the Court.

(3) *Party Witnesses:* A party may take the deposition of another party without the consent of all the parties as follows:

(A) *Motion:* A party desiring to depose another party shall file a written motion which shall state that the deposition is to be taken under Rule 74(c)(3) and shall set forth the name of the person to be deposed, the time and place of the deposition, and the officer before whom the deposition is to be taken. With respect to the deposition of an organization described in Rule 81(c), the motion shall also set forth the information required under that Rule, and the organization shall make the designation authorized by that Rule.

(B) *Objection:* Upon the filing of a motion to take the deposition of a party, the Court shall issue an order directing each non-moving party to file a written objec- tion or response thereto.

(C) *Action by the Court Sua Sponte:* In the exercise of its discretion the Court may on its own motion order the taking of a deposition of a party witness and may in its order allocate the cost therefor as it deems appro- priate.

(4) *Expert Witnesses:* A party may take the deposition of an expert witness without the consent of all the parties as follows:

(A) *Scope of Deposition:* The deposition of an expert witness under this subparagraph shall be limited to: (i) The knowledge, skill, experience, training, or education that qualifies the witness to testify as an expert in re- spect of the issue or issues in dispute, (ii) the opinion of the witness in respect of which the witness's expert testi- mony is relevant to the issue or issues in dispute, (iii) the facts or data that underlie that opinion, and (iv) the witness's analysis, showing how the witness proceeded from the facts or data to draw the conclusion that rep- resents the opinion of the witness.

(B) *Procedure:* (i) *General:* A party desiring to de- pose an expert witness under this subparagraph (4) shall file a written motion and shall set forth therein the mat- ters specified below:

(a) The name and address of the witness to be examined;

(b) a statement describing any books, papers, documents, electronically stored information, or tan- gible things to be produced at the deposition of the witness to be examined;

(c)   a statement of issues in controversy to which the expected testimony of the expert witness, or the document, electronically stored information, or thing relates, and the reasons for deposing the witness;

(d)   the time and place proposed for the deposition;

(e)   the officer before whom the deposition is to be taken;

(f)   any provision desired with respect to the payment of the costs, expenses, fees, and charges relat- ing to the deposition (see paragraph (c)(4)(D)); and

(g)   if the movant proposes to video record the deposition, then a statement to that effect and the name and address of the video recorder operator and the operator's employer. (The video recorder operator and the officer before whom the deposition is to be taken may be the same person.)

The movant shall also show that prior notice of the mo- tion has been given to the expert witness whose deposi- tion is sought and to each other party, or counsel for each other party, and shall state the position of each of these persons with respect to the motion, in accordance with Rule 50(a).

(ii) *Disposition of Motion:* Any objection or other response to the motion for order to depose an expert witness under this subparagraph shall be filed with the Court within 15 days after service of the motion.   If the Court approves the taking of a deposition, then   it will issue an order as described in paragraph (e)(4) of this Rule. If the deposition is to be video recorded, then the Court's order will so state.

(C)   *Action by the Court Sua Sponte:*   In the exercise of its discretion the Court may on its own motion order the taking of a deposition of an expert witness and may   in its order allocate the cost therefor as it deems appro- priate.

(D)   *Expenses:* (i) *In General:* By stipulation among the parties and the expert witness to be deposed, or on order of the Court, provision may be made for any costs, expenses, fees, or charges relating to the deposi- tion. If there is not such a stipulation or order, then the costs, expenses, fees, and charges relating to the deposi- tion shall be borne by the parties as set forth in para- graph (c)(4)(D)(ii).

(ii) *Allocation of Costs, Etc.:* The party taking the deposition shall pay the following costs, expenses, fees, and charges:

(a)   A reasonable fee for the expert witness, with regard to the usual and customary charge of the wit- ness, for the time spent in preparing for and attend- ing the deposition;

(b)   reasonable charges of the expert witness for

53

models, samples, or other like matters that may be required in the deposition of the witness;

(c) such amounts as are allowable under Rule 148(a) for transportation and subsistence for the expert witness;

(d) any charges of the officer presiding at or recording the deposition (other than for copies of the deposition transcript);

(e) any expenses involved in providing a place for the deposition; and

(f) the cost for the original of the deposition transcript as well as for any copies thereof that the party taking the deposition might order.

The other parties and the expert witness shall pay the cost for any copies of the deposition transcript that they might order.

(iii) *Failure To Attend:* If the party authorized to take the deposition of the expert witness fails to at- tend or to proceed therewith, then the Court may order that party to pay the witness such fees, charges, and expenses that the witness would otherwise be en- titled to under paragraph (c)(4)(D)(ii) and to pay any other party such expenses, including attorney's fees, that the Court deems reasonable under the cir- cumstances.

(d) Use of Deposition of an Expert Witness for Other Than Discovery Purposes: (1) *Use as Expert Wit- ness Report:* Upon written motion by the proponent of the expert witness and in appropriate cases, the Court may order that the deposition transcript serve as the expert witness re- port required by Rule 143(g)(1). Unless the Court shall deter- mine otherwise for good cause shown, the taking of a deposi- tion of an expert witness will not serve to extend the date under Rule 143(g)(1) by which a party is required to furnish to each other party and to submit to the Court a copy of all expert witness reports prepared pursuant to that Rule.

(2) *Other Use:* Any other use of a deposition of an expert witness shall be governed by the provisions of Rule 81(i).

(e) General Provisions: Depositions taken under this Rule are subject to the following provisions. (1) *Transcript:* A transcript shall be made of every deposition upon oral examination taken under this Rule, but the transcript and ex- hibits introduced in connection with the deposition generally shall not be filed with the Court. See Rule 81(h)(3).

(2) *Depositions Upon Written Questions:* Depositions under this Rule may be taken upon written questions rather than upon oral examination. If the deposition is to be taken on written questions, a copy of the written questions shall be annexed to the notice of deposition or motion to take deposition. The use of such written questions is not favored, and the deposition should not be taken in this manner in the absence of a special reason. See Rule 84(a). There shall be an

opportunity for cross-questions and redi-rect questions to the same extent and within the same time periods as provided in Rule 84(b) (starting with serv-ice of a notice of or motion to take deposition rather than service of an application). With respect to taking the depo-sition, the procedure of Rule 84(c) shall apply.

[1](3) *Hearing:* A hearing on a motion for an order regarding a deposition under this Rule will be held only if directed by the Court. A motion for an order regarding a deposition may be granted by the Court to the extent consistent with Rule 70(c)(1).

(4) *Orders:* If the Court approves the taking of a deposition under this Rule, then it will issue an order which includes in its terms the name of the person to be examined, the time and place of the deposition, and the officer before whom it is to be taken.

(5) *Continuances:* Unless the Court shall determine otherwise for good cause shown, the taking of a deposition under this Rule will not be regarded as sufficient ground for granting a continuance from a date or place of trial theretofore set.

Other Applicable Rules: Unless otherwise pro-vided in this Rule, the depositions described in this Rule generally shall be governed by the provisions of the following Rules with respect to the matters to which they apply: Rule 81(c) (designation of person to testify), 81(e) (person before whom deposition taken), 81(f) (taking of deposition), 81(g) (expenses), 81(h) (execution, form, and return of deposition), 81(i) (use of deposition), and Rule 85 (objections, errors, and irregularities). For Rules concerned with the timing and frequency of depositions, supplementation of answers, protective orders, effect of evasive or incomplete answers or responses, and sanctions and enforcement action, see Title X. For provisions governing the issuance of subpoenas, see Rule 147(d).

TITLE VIII DEPOSITIONS TO PERPETUATE EVIDENCE 1

RULE 80. GENERAL PROVISIONS

[2](a) **General:** On complying with the applicable requirements, depositions to perpetuate evidence may be taken in a pending case before trial (Rule 81), or in anticipation of commencing a case in this Court (Rule 82), or in connection with the trial (Rule 83). Depositions under this Title may be taken only for the purpose of making testimony or any document, electronically stored information, or thing available as evidence in the circumstances herein authorized by the applicable Rules. Depositions for discovery purposes may be taken only in accordance with Rule 74.

(b) **Other Applicable Rules:** For Rules concerned with the timing and frequency of depositions, supplementation of answers, protective orders, effect of evasive or incomplete answers or responses, and sanctions and enforcement action, see Title X. For provisions relating to tender of fees and other amounts to the witness to be deposed, see Rule 148(b).

RULE 81. DEPOSITIONS IN PENDING CASE [3]

(a) Depositions To Perpetuate Testimony: A party to a case pending in the Court, who desires to perpetuate testimony or to preserve any document, electronically stored information, or thing, shall file an application pursuant to these Rules for an order of the Court authorizing such party to take a deposition for such purpose. Such depositions shall be taken only where there is a substantial risk that the person or document, electronically stored information, or thing involved will not be available at the trial of the case, and shall relate only to testimony or document, electronically stored information, or thing which is not privileged and is material to a matter in controversy.

(b) The Application: (1) *Content of Application:* The application to take a deposition pursuant to paragraph (a) of this Rule shall be signed by the party seeking the deposition or such party's counsel, and shall show the following:

(A) The names and addresses of the persons to be examined;

(B) the reasons for deposing those persons rather than waiting to call them as witnesses at the trial;

(C) the substance of the testimony which the party expects to elicit from each of those persons;

(D) a statement showing how the proposed testimony or document, electronically stored information, or thing is material to a matter in controversy;

(E) a statement describing any books, papers, documents, electronically stored information, or tangible things to be produced at the deposition by the persons to be examined;

(F) the time and place proposed for the deposition;

(G) the officer before whom the deposition is to be taken;

(H) the date on which the petition was filed with the Court, and whether the pleadings have been closed and the case placed on a trial calendar;

(I) any provision desired with respect to payment of expenses, fees, and charges relating to the deposition (see paragraph (g) of this Rule, and Rule 103); and

(J) if the applicant proposes to video record the deposition, then the application shall so state, and shall show the name and address of the video recorder operator and of the operator's employer. (The video recorder operator and the officer before whom the deposition is to be taken may be the same person. See subparagraph (2) of paragraph (j) of this Rule.)

The application shall also have annexed to it a copy of the questions to be propounded, if the deposition is to be taken on written questions. For the form of application to take a deposition, see Appendix I.

(2) *Filing and Disposition of Application:* The application may be filed with the Court at any time after the case is docketed in the Court, but must be filed at least 45 days prior to the date set for the trial of the case. The application and a conformed copy thereof, together with an additional conformed copy for each additional docket number involved, shall be filed with the Clerk. In addition to serving each of the other parties to the case, the applicant shall serve a copy of the application on such other persons who are to be examined pursuant to the application, and shall file with the Clerk a certificate showing such service. Such other parties or persons shall file their objections or other response, with the same number of copies and with a certificate of service thereof on the other parties and such other persons, within 15 days after such service of the application. A hearing on the application will be held only if directed by the Court. Unless the Court shall determine otherwise for good cause shown, an application to take a deposition will not be regarded as sufficient ground for granting a continuance from a date or place of trial theretofore set. If the Court approves the taking of a deposition, then it will issue an order which will include in its terms the name of the person to be examined, the time and place of the deposition, and the officer before whom it is to be taken. If the deposition is to be video recorded, then the Court's order will so state.

(c) Designation of Person To Testify: The party seeking to take a deposition may name, as the deponent in the application, a public or private corporation or a partner- ship or association or governmental agency, and shall designate with reasonable particularity the matters on which ex- amination is requested. The organization so named shall designate one or more officers, directors, or managing agents, or other persons who consent to testify on its behalf, and may set forth, for each person designated, the matters on which such person will testify. The persons so designated shall testify as to matters known or reasonably available to the organization.

(d) Use of Stipulation: The parties or their counsel may execute and file a stipulation to take a deposition by agreement instead of filing an application as herein above provided. Such a stipulation shall be filed with the Court in duplicate, and shall contain the same information as is required in items (A), (F), (G), (I), and (J) of Rule 81(b)(1), but shall not require the approval or an order of the Court unless the effect is to delay the trial of the case. A deposition taken pursuant to a stipulation shall in all respects conform to the requirements of these Rules.

(e) Person Before Whom Deposition Taken: (1) *Domestic Depositions:* Within the United States or a territory or insular possession subject to the dominion of the United States, depositions shall be taken before an officer authorized to administer oaths by the laws of the United States (see Code section 7622) or of the place where the examination is held, or before a person appointed by the Court. A person so appointed has power to administer oaths and to take such testimony.

(2) *Foreign Depositions:* In a foreign country, depositions may be taken: (A) Before a person authorized to ad- minister oaths or affirmations in the place in which the ex- amination is held, either by the law thereof or by the law of the United States; (B) before a person commissioned by the Court, and a person so commissioned shall have the power, by virtue of the commission, to administer any necessary oath and take testimony; or (C) pursuant to a letter rogatory or a letter of request issued in accordance with the provisions of the Hague Convention of 18 March 1970 on the Taking of Evidence Abroad in Civil or Commercial Matters, Mar. 18, 1970, 23 U.S.T. (Part 3) 2555. A commission, a letter rogatory, or a letter of request shall be issued on application and notice and on terms that are just and appropriate. The party seeking to take a foreign deposition shall contact the United States Department of State to as- certain any requirements imposed by it or by the foreign country in which the deposition is to be taken, including any required foreign language translations and any fees or costs, and shall submit to the Court, along with the appli- cation, any such foreign language translations, fees, costs, or other materials required. It is not requisite to the issuance of a commission, a letter rogatory, or a letter of request that the taking of the deposition in any other manner be impracticable or inconvenient; and both a commission and a letter rogatory, or both a commission and a letter of request, may be issued in proper cases. A notice or commission may designate the person before whom the deposition is to be taken either by name or descriptive title. A letter rogatory may be addressed "To the Appropriate Authority in [here name the country]." A letter of request is addressed to the central authority of the requested State. The model recommended for letters of request is set forth in the Hague Convention of 18 March 1970 on the Taking of Evidence Abroad in Civil or Commercial Matters. Evidence obtained by deposition or in response to a letter rogatory or a letter of request need not be excluded merely for the reason that it is not a verbatim transcript or that the testimony was not taken under oath or for any similar departure from the requirements for depositions within the United States under these Rules.

(3) *Disqualification for Interest:* No deposition shall be taken before a person who is a relative or employee or

counsel of any party, or is a relative or employee or associate of such counsel, or is financially interested in the action. However, on consent of all the parties or their counsel, a deposition may be taken before such person, but only if the relationship of that person and the waiver are set forth in the certificate of return to the Court.

(f) Taking of Deposition: (1) *Arrangements:* All arrangements necessary for taking of the deposition shall be made by the party filing the application or, in the case of a stipulation, by such other persons as may be agreed upon by the parties.

(2) *Procedure:* Attendance by the persons to be examined may be compelled by the issuance of a subpoena, and production likewise may be compelled of exhibits required in connection with the testimony being taken. The officer before whom the deposition is taken shall first put the witness on oath (or affirmation) and shall personally, or by someone acting under such officer's direction and in such officer's presence, record accurately and verbatim the questions asked, the answers given, the objections made, and all matters transpiring at the taking of the deposition which bear on the testimony involved. Examination and cross-examination of witnesses, and the marking of exhibits, shall proceed as permitted at trial. All objections made at the time of examination shall be noted by the officer upon the deposition. Evidence objected to, unless privileged, shall be taken subject to the objections made. If an answer is improperly refused and as a result a further deposition is taken by the interrogating party, the objecting party or deponent may be required to pay all costs, charges, and expenses of that deposition to the same ex- tent as is provided in paragraph (g) of this Rule where a party seeking to take a deposition fails to appear at the taking of the deposition. At the request of either party, a prospective witness at the deposition, other than a person acting in an expert or advisory capacity for a party, shall be excluded from the room in which, and during the time that, the testimony of another witness is being taken; and if such person remains in the room or within hearing of the examination after such request has been made, such per- son shall not thereafter be permitted to testify, except by the consent of the party who requested such person's exclusion or by permission of the Court.

(g) Expenses: (1) *General:* The party taking the deposition shall pay all the expenses, fees, and charges of the witness whose deposition is taken by such party, any charges of the officer presiding at or recording the deposition other than for copies of the deposition, and any expenses involved in providing a place for the deposition. The party taking the deposition shall pay for the original of the deposition; and, upon payment of reasonable charges therefor, the officer shall also furnish a copy of the deposition to any party or the deponent. By stipulation between the parties or on order of the Court, provision may be made for any costs, charges, or expenses relating to the deposition.

(2) *Failure To Attend or To Serve Subpoena:* If the party authorized to take a deposition fails to attend and proceed therewith and another party attends in person or by attorney pursuant to the arrangements made, then the Court may order the former party to pay to such other party the reasonable expenses incurred by such other party and such other party's attorney in attending, including reasonable attorney's fees. If the party authorized to take a deposition of a witness fails to serve a subpoena upon the witness and the witness because of such failure does not attend, and if another party attends in person or by attorney because such party expects the deposition of that wit- ness to be taken, then the Court may order the former party to pay to such other party the reasonable expenses incurred by such other party and such other party's attorney attending, including reasonable attorney's fees.

(h)   Execution and Return of Deposition: (1) *Sub- mission to Witness; Changes; Signing:* When the testimony is fully transcribed, the deposition shall be submitted to the witness for examination and shall be read to or by the wit- ness, unless such examination and reading are waived by the witness and by the parties. Any changes in form or sub- stance, which the witness desires to make, shall be entered upon the deposition by the officer with a statement of the reasons given by the witness for making them. The deposition shall then be signed by the witness, unless the parties   by stipulation waive the signing or the witness is ill or can- not be found or refuses to sign. If the deposition is not signed by the witness within 30 days of its submission to the wit- ness, then the officer shall sign it and state on the record the fact of the waiver or of the illness or absence of the witness or the fact of the refusal to sign together with the reason, if any, given therefor; and the deposition may then be used as fully as though signed unless the Court determines that the reasons given for the refusal to sign require rejection of the deposition in whole or in part. As to correction of errors, see Rules 85 and 143(d).

(2)   *Form:* The deposition shall show the docket number and caption of the case as they appear in the Court's records, the place and date of taking the deposition, the name of the witness, the party by whom called, and the names of counsel present and whom they represent. The pages of the deposition shall be securely fastened. Exhibits shall be carefully marked, and when practicable annexed to, and in any event returned with, the deposition, unless, upon motion to the Court, a copy shall be permitted as a substitute after an opportunity is given to all interested parties to examine and

compare the original and the copy. The officer shall execute and attach to the deposition a certificate in accordance with Form 16 shown in Appendix I.

(3) *Return of Deposition:* The deposition and exhibits shall not be filed with the Court. Unless otherwise directed by the Court, the officer shall deliver the original deposition and exhibits to the party taking the deposition or such party's counsel, who shall take custody of and be responsible for the safeguarding of the original deposition and exhibits. Upon payment of reasonable charges therefor, the officer also shall deliver a copy of the deposition and exhibits to any party or the deponent, or to counsel for any party or for the deponent. As to use of a deposition at the trial or in any other proceeding in the case, see paragraph

(i) of this Rule. As to introduction of a deposition in evidence, see Rule 143(d).

(i) Use of Deposition: At the trial or in any other proceeding in the case, any part or all of a deposition, so far as admissible under the rules of evidence applied as though the witness were then present and testifying, may be used against any party who was present or represented at the taking of the deposition or who had reasonable notice thereof, in accordance with any of the following provisions:

(1) The deposition may be used by any party for the purpose of contradicting or impeaching the testimony of the deponent as a witness.

(2) The deposition of a party may be used by an adverse party for any purpose.

(3) The deposition may be used for any purpose if the Court finds: (A) That the witness is dead; (B) that the witness is at such distance from the place of trial that it is not practicable for the witness to attend, unless it appears that the absence of the witness was procured by the party seeking to use the deposition; (C) that the witness is unable to attend or testify because of age, illness, infirmity, or imprisonment; (D) that the party offering the deposition has been unable to obtain attendance of the witness at the trial, as to make it desirable in the interests of justice, to allow the deposition to be used; or (E) that such exceptional circumstances exist, in regard to the absence of the witness at the trial, as to make it desirable in the interests of justice, to allow the deposition to be used.

(4) If only part of a deposition is offered in evidence by a party, then an adverse party may require the party offering the deposition to introduce any other part which ought in fairness to be considered with the part introduced, and any party may introduce any other parts. As to introduction of a deposition in evidence, see Rule 143(d).

(j) Video Recorded Depositions: (1) *General:* By stipulation of the parties or upon order of the Court, a deposition to perpetuate testimony to be taken upon oral examination may be video recorded. Except as otherwise provided

by this paragraph, all other provisions of these Rules governing the practice and procedure in depositions shall apply.

(2) *Procedure:* The deposition shall begin by the operator stating on camera: (A) The operator's name and address; (B) the name and address of the operator's employer; (C) the date, time, and place of the deposition; (D) the caption and docket number of the case; (E) the name of the witness; and (F) the party on whose behalf the deposition is being taken. The officer before whom the deposition is taken shall then identify himself or herself and swear the witness on camera. At the conclusion of the deposition, the operator shall state on camera that the deposition is concluded. The officer before whom the deposition is taken and the operator may be the same person. When the deposition spans multiple units of video storage medium (tape, disc, etc.), the end of each unit and the beginning of each succeeding unit shall be announced on camera by the operator. The deposition shall be timed by a digital clock on camera which shall show continually each hour, minute, and second of the deposition.

(3) *Transcript:* If requested by one of the parties, then the testimony shall be transcribed at the cost of such party; but no signature of the witness shall be required, and the transcript shall not be filed with the Court.

(4) *Custody:* The party taking the deposition or such party's counsel shall take custody of and be responsible for the safeguarding of the video recording together with any exhibits, and such party shall permit the viewing of or shall provide a copy of the video recording and any exhibits upon the request and at the cost of any other party.

(5) *Use:* A video recorded deposition may be used at a trial or hearing in the manner and to the extent provided in paragraph (i) of this Rule. The party who offers the video recording in evidence shall provide all necessary equipment for viewing the video recording and personnel to operate such equipment. At a trial or hearing, that part of the audio portion of a video recorded deposition which is offered in evidence and admitted, or which is excluded on objection, shall be transcribed in the same manner as the testimony of other witnesses. The video recording shall be marked as an exhibit and, subject to the provisions of Rule 143(e)(2), shall remain in the custody of the Court.

RULE 82. DEPOSITIONS BEFORE COMMENCEMENT OF CASE[1]

A person who desires to perpetuate testimony or to pre-serve any document, electronically stored information, or thing regarding any matter that may be cognizable in this Court may file an application with the Court to take a deposition for such purpose. The application shall be entitled in the name of the applicant, shall otherwise be in the same style and form as apply to a motion filed with the Court, and shall show the following: (1) The facts showing that the applicant expects to be a party to a case cognizable in this Court but is at present unable to bring it or cause it to be brought; (2) the subject matter of the expected action and the applicant's interest therein; and (3) all matters required to be shown in an application under paragraph (b)(1) of Rule 81 except item (H) thereof. Such an application will be entered upon a special docket, and service thereof and pleading with respect thereto will proceed subject to the requirements otherwise applicable to a motion. A hearing on the application may be required by the Court. If the Court is satisfied that the perpetuation of the testimony or the preservation of the document, electronically stored information, or thing may prevent a failure or delay of justice, then it will make an order authorizing the deposition and including such other terms and conditions as it may deem appropriate consistently with these Rules. If the deposition is taken, and if thereafter the expected case is commenced in this Court, then the depo- sition may be used in that case subject to the Rules which would apply if the deposition had been taken after commencement of the case.

RULE 83. DEPOSITIONS AFTER COMMENCEMENT OF TRIAL

Nothing in these Rules shall preclude the taking of a deposition after trial has commenced in a case, upon approval or direction of the Court. The Court may impose such conditions to the taking of the deposition as it may find appropriate and, with respect to any aspect not provided for by the Court, Rule 81 shall govern to the extent applicable.

RULE 84. DEPOSITIONS UPON WRITTEN QUESTIONS

(a) Use of Written Questions: A party may make an application to the Court to take a deposition, otherwise authorized under Rule 81, 82, or 83, upon written questions rather than oral examination. The provisions of those Rules shall apply in all respects to such a deposition except to the extent clearly inapplicable or otherwise provided in this Rule. Unless there is special reason for taking the deposition on written questions rather than oral examination, the Court will deny the application, without prejudice to seeking approval of the deposition upon oral examination. The taking of depositions upon written questions is not favored, except when the deposition is to be taken in a foreign country, in which event the deposition must be taken on written questions unless otherwise directed by the Court for good cause shown.

(b) Procedure: An application under paragraph (a) hereof shall have the written questions annexed thereto. With respect to such application, the 15-day period for filing objections prescribed by paragraph (b)(2) of Rule 81 is extended to 20 days, and within that 20-day period the objecting or responding party shall also file with the Court any cross-questions which such party may desire to be asked at the taking of the deposition. The applicant shall then file any objections to the cross-questions, as well as any redirect questions, within 15 days after service on the applicant of the cross-questions. Within 15 days after service of the redirect questions on the other party, the other party shall file with the Court any objections to the redirect questions, as well as any recross-questions which the other party may de- sire to be asked. No objection to a written question will be considered unless it is filed with the Court within such applicable time. An original and five copies of all questions and objections shall be filed with the Clerk, who will make service thereof on the opposite party. The Court for good cause shown may enlarge or shorten the time in any respect.

(c) Taking of Deposition: The officer taking the deposition shall propound all questions to the witness in their proper order. The parties and their counsel may attend the taking of the deposition but shall not participate in the deposition proceeding in any manner.

(d) Execution and Return: The execution and return of the deposition shall conform to the requirements of paragraph (h) of Rule 81.

RULE 85. OBJECTIONS, ERRORS, AND IRREGULARITIES

(a) As to Initiating Deposition: All errors and irregularities in the procedure for obtaining approval for the taking of a deposition are waived unless made in writing within the time for making objections or promptly where no time is prescribed.

(b) As to Disqualification of Officer: Objection to taking a deposition because of disqualification of the officer before whom it is to be taken is waived unless made before the taking of the deposition begins or as soon thereafter as the disqualification becomes known or could be discovered with reasonable diligence.

(c) As to Use: In general, an objection may be made at the trial or hearing to use of a deposition, in whole or in part as evidence, for any reason which would require the exclusion of the testimony as evidence if the witness were then present and testifying. However, objections to the competency of a witness or to the competency, relevancy, or materiality of testimony are waived by failure to make them before or during the taking of the deposition, if the ground of the objection is one which might have been obviated or removed if presented at that time.

(d) As to Manner and Form: Errors and irregularities occurring at the oral examination in the manner of taking the deposition, in the form of the questions or answers, in the oath or affirmation, or in the conduct of the parties, and errors of any kind which might have been obviated, removed, or cured if promptly presented, are waived unless reasonable objection thereto is made at the taking of the deposition.

[1]**(e) As to Errors by Officer:** Errors or irregularities in the manner in which testimony is transcribed or the deposition is prepared, signed, certified, sealed, endorsed, transmitted, filed, or otherwise dealt with by the presiding officer, are waived unless a motion to correct or suppress the deposition or some part thereof is made with reasonable promptness after such defect is, or with due diligence might have been, ascertained. See also Rule 143(d).

TITLE IX

ADMISSIONS AND STIPULATIONS

RULE 90. REQUESTS FOR ADMISSIONS

(a) Scope and Time of Request: A party may serve upon any other party a written request for the admission, for purposes of the pending action only, of the truth of any matters which are not privileged and are relevant to the subject matter involved in the pending action, but only if such matters are set forth in the request and relate to statements or opinions of fact or of the application of law to fact, including the genuineness of any documents described in the request. However, the Court expects the parties to attempt to attain the objectives of such a request through informal consultation or communication before utilizing the procedures provided in this Rule. Requests for admission shall not be commenced, without leave of Court, before the expiration of 30 days after joinder of issue (see Rule 38). Requests for admission shall be completed and any motion to review under paragraph (e) hereof shall be filed, unless otherwise authorized by the Court, no later than 45 days prior to the date set for call of the case from a trial calendar.

(b) The Request: The request may, without leave of Court, be served by any party to a pending case. The request shall separately set forth each matter of which an admission is requested and shall advise the party to whom the request is directed of the consequences of failing to respond as pro- vided by paragraph (c). Copies of documents shall be served with the request unless they have been or are otherwise furnished or made available for inspection and copying. The party making the request shall simultaneously serve a copy thereof on the other party and file the original with proof of service with the Court.

(c)   Response to Request: Each matter is deemed ad- mitted unless, within 30 days after service of the request or within such shorter or longer time as the Court may allow,   the party to whom the request is directed serves upon the re- questing party: (1) A written answer specifically admitting or   denying the matter involved in whole or in part, or asserting that it cannot be truthfully admitted or denied and setting forth in detail the reasons why this is so; or (2) an objection, stating in detail the reasons therefor. The response shall be signed by the party or the party's counsel, and the original thereof, with proof of service on the other party, shall be filed with the Court. A denial shall fairly meet the substance of   the requested admission, and, when good faith requires that   a party qualify an answer or deny only a part of a matter,   such party shall specify so much of it as is true and deny or   qualify the remainder. An answering party may not give lack of information or knowledge as a reason for failure to admit or deny unless such party states that such party has made reasonable inquiry and that the information known or readily obtainable by such party is insufficient to enable such party to admit or deny. A party who considers that a matter,   of which an admission has been requested, presents a genuine issue for trial may not, on that ground alone, object to the request; such party may, subject to the provisions of paragraph (g) of this Rule, deny the matter or set forth rea- sons why such party cannot admit or deny it. An objection   on the ground of relevance may be noted by any party but   it is not to be regarded as just cause for refusal to admit or deny.

(d)   Effect of Signature: (1) The signature of counsel   or a party constitutes a certification that the signer has read   the request for admission or response or objection, and that   to the best of the signer's knowledge, information, and belief formed after a reasonable inquiry, it is: (A) Consistent with these Rules and warranted by existing law or a good faith argument for the extension, modification, or reversal of existing law; (B) not interposed for any improper purpose, such as to harass or to cause unnecessary delay or needless increase in the cost of litigation; and (C) not unreasonable or unduly burdensome or expensive, given the needs of the case, the discovery already had in the case, the amount in controversy, and the importance of the issues at stake in the litigation. If a request, response, or objection is not signed, it shall be stricken, unless it is signed promptly after the omission is called to the attention of the party making the request, response, or objection, and a party shall not be obligated to   take any action with respect to it until it is signed.

(2) If a certification is made in violation of this Rule, the Court, upon motion or upon its own initiative, may impose upon the person who made the certification, the party on whose behalf the request, response, or objection is made, or both, an appropriate sanction, which may include an order to pay the amount of the reasonable expenses incurred because of the violation, including reasonable counsel's fees.

(e) Motion To Review: The party who has requested the admissions may move to determine the sufficiency of the answers or objections. Unless the Court determines that an objection is justified, it shall order that an answer be served. If the Court determines that an answer does not comply with the requirements of this Rule, then it may order either that the matter is admitted or that an amended answer be served. In lieu of any such order, the Court may determine that final disposition of the request shall be made at some later time which may be more appropriate for disposing of the question involved.

(f) Effect of Admission: Any matter admitted under this Rule is conclusively established unless the Court on motion permits withdrawal or modification of the admission. Subject to any other orders made in the case by the Court, withdrawal or modification may be permitted when the presentation of the merits of the case will be subserved thereby, and the party who obtained the admission fails to satisfy the Court that the withdrawal or modification will prejudice such party in prosecuting such party's case or defense on the merits. Any admission made by a party under this Rule is for the purpose of the pending action only and is not an admission by such party for any other purpose, nor may it be used against such party in any other proceeding.

(g) Sanctions: If any party unjustifiably fails to admit the genuineness of any document or the truth of any matter as requested in accordance with this Rule, the party requesting the admission may apply to the Court for an order imposing such sanction on the other party or the other party's counsel as the Court may find appropriate in the circumstances, including but not limited to the sanctions pro- vided in Title X. The failure to admit may be found unjustifiable unless the Court finds that: (1) The request was held objectionable pursuant to this Rule, (2) the admission sought was of no substantial importance, (3) the party failing to admit had reasonable ground to doubt the truth of the mat- ter or the genuineness of the document in respect of which
the admission was sought, or (4) there was other good reason for failure to admit.

(h) Other Applicable Rules: For Rules concerned with frequency and timing of requests for admission in relation to other procedures, supplementation of answers, effect of evasive or incomplete answers or responses, protective orders, and sanctions and enforcement action, see Title X.

RULE 91. STIPULATIONS FOR TRIAL

(a) Stipulations Required: (1) *General:* The parties are required to stipulate, to the fullest extent to which complete or qualified agreement can or fairly should be reached, all matters not privileged which are relevant to the pending case, regardless of whether such matters involve fact or opinion or the application of law to fact. Included in matters required to be stipulated are all facts, all documents and papers or contents or aspects thereof, and all evidence which fairly should not be in dispute. Where the truth or authenticity of facts or evidence claimed to be relevant by one party is not disputed, an objection on the ground of materiality or relevance may be noted by any other party but is not to be regarded as just cause for refusal to stipulate. The requirement of stipulation applies under this Rule without regard to where the burden of proof may lie with respect to the matters involved. Documents or papers or other exhibits annexed to or filed with the stipulation shall be considered to be part of the stipulation.

[1](2) *Stipulations To Be Comprehensive:* The fact that any matter may have been obtained through discovery or requests for admission or through any other authorized procedure is not grounds for omitting such matter from the stipulation. Such procedures should be regarded as aids to stipulation, and matter obtained through them which is within the scope of subparagraph (1) must be set forth comprehensively in the stipulation, in logical order in the context of all other provisions of the stipulation. A failure to include in the stipulation a matter admitted under Rule 90(f) does not affect the Court's ability to consider such ad- mitted matter.

Form: Stipulations required under this Rule shall be in writing, signed by the parties thereto or by their counsel, and shall observe the requirements of Rule 23 as to form and style of papers, except that the stipulation shall be filed with the Court in duplicate and only one set of exhibits shall be required. Documents or other papers, which are the subject of stipulation in any respect and which the parties in- tend to place before the Court, shall be annexed to or filed with the stipulation. The stipulation shall be clear and concise. Separate items shall be stated in separate paragraphs, and shall be appropriately lettered or numbered. Exhibits attached to a stipulation shall be numbered serially; i.e., 1, 2, 3, etc. The exhibit number shall be followed by ''P'' if offered by the petitioner, e.g., 1–P; ''R'' if offered by the respondent, e.g., 2–R; or ''J'' if joint, e.g., 3–J.

(b) Filing: Executed stipulations prepared pursuant to this Rule, and related exhibits, shall be filed by the parties at or before commencement of the trial of the case, unless the Court in the particular case shall otherwise specify. A stipulation when filed need not be offered formally to be considered in evidence.

(c) Objections: Any objection to all or any part of a stipulation should be noted in the stipulation, but the Court will consider any objection to a stipulated matter made at the commencement of the trial or for good cause shown made during the trial.

(d) Binding Effect: A stipulation shall be treated, to the extent of its terms, as a conclusive admission by the par- ties to the stipulation, unless otherwise permitted by the Court or agreed upon by those parties. The Court will not permit a party to a stipulation to qualify, change, or contradict a stipulation in whole or in part, except that it may do so where justice requires. A stipulation and the admissions therein shall be binding and have effect only in the pending case and not for any other purpose, and cannot be used against any of the parties thereto in any other case or proceeding.

(f) Noncompliance by a Party: (1) *Motion To Compel Stipulation:* If, after the date of issuance of trial notice in a case, a party has refused or failed to confer with an adversary with respect to entering into a stipulation in accordance with this Rule, or a party has refused or failed to make such a stipulation of any matter within the terms of this Rule, the party proposing to stipulate may, at a time not later than 45 days prior to the date set for call of the case from a trial calendar, file a motion with the Court for an order directing the delinquent party to show cause why the matters covered in the motion should not be deemed admit- ted for the purposes of the case. The motion shall: (A) Show with particularity and by separately numbered paragraphs each matter which is claimed for stipulation; (B) set forth in express language the specific stipulation which the moving party proposes with respect to each such matter and annex thereto or make available to the Court and the other parties each document or other paper as to which the moving party desires a stipulation; (C) set forth the sources, reasons, and basis for claiming, with respect to each such matter, that it should be stipulated; and (D) show that opposing counsel or the other parties have had reasonable access to those sources or basis for stipulation and have been informed of the rea- sons for stipulation.

(2) *Procedure:* Upon the filing of such a motion, an order to show cause as moved shall be issued forthwith, unless the Court shall direct otherwise. The order to show cause will be served by the Clerk, with a copy thereof sent to the moving party. Within 20 days of the service of the order to show cause, the party to whom the order is directed shall file a response with the Court, with proof of service of a copy thereof on opposing counsel or the other parties, showing why the matters set forth in the motion papers should not be deemed admitted for purposes of the pending case. The response shall list each matter involved on which there is no

dispute, referring specifically to the numbered paragraphs in the motion to which the admissions relate. Where a matter is disputed only in part, the response shall show the part admitted and the part disputed. Where the responding party is willing to stipulate   in whole or in part with respect to any matter in the motion by varying or qualifying a matter in the proposed stipulation, the response shall set forth the variance or qualification and the admission which the responding party is willing to make. Where the response claims that there is a dispute as to any matter in part or in whole, or where the response presents a variance or qualification with respect to any matter in the motion, the response shall show the sources, reasons, and basis on which the responding party relies for that purpose. The Court, where it is found appropriate, may set the order to show cause for a hearing or conference at such time as the Court shall determine.

(3) *Failure of Response:* If no response is filed within the period specified with respect to any matter or portion thereof, or if the response is evasive or not fairly directed   to the proposed stipulation or portion thereof, that matter   or portion thereof will be deemed stipulated for purposes   of the pending case, and an order will be issued accordingly.

(4) *Matters Considered:* Opposing claims of evidence will not be weighed under this Rule unless such evidence   is patently incredible. Nor will a genuinely controverted or doubtful issue of fact be determined in advance of trial. The Court will determine whether a genuine dispute exists, or whether in the interests of justice a matter ought   not be deemed stipulated.

RULE 92. CASES CONSOLIDATED FOR TRIAL

With respect to a common matter in cases consolidated for trial, the reference to a "party" in this Title IX or in Title X shall mean any party to any of the consolidated cases involving such common matter.

GENERAL PROVISIONS GOVERNING DISCOVERY, DEPOSITIONS, AND REQUESTS FOR ADMISSION

RULE 100. APPLICABILITY [1]

The Rules in this Title apply according to their terms to written interrogatories (Rule 71), production of documents, electronically stored information, or things (Rule 72), examination by transferees (Rule 73), depositions (Rules 74, 81, 82, 83, and 84), and requests for admission (Rule 90). Such procedures may be used in anticipation of the stipulation of facts required by Rule 91, but the existence of such proce- dures or their use does not excuse failure to comply with the requirements of that Rule. See Rule 91(a)(2).

RULE 101. SEQUENCE, TIMING, AND FREQUENCY

Unless the Court orders otherwise for the convenience of the parties and witnesses and in the interests of justice, and subject to the provisions of the Rules herein which apply more specifically, the procedures set forth in Rule 100 may be used in any sequence, and the fact that a party is engaged in any such method or procedure shall not operate to delay the use of any such method or procedure by any other party. However, none of these methods or procedures shall be used in a manner or at a time which shall delay or impede the progress of the case toward trial status or the trial of the case on the date for which it is noticed, unless in the interests of justice the Court shall order otherwise. Unless the Court orders otherwise under Rule 103, the frequency of use of these methods or procedures is not limited.

RULE 102. SUPPLEMENTATION OF RESPONSES[2]

A party who has responded to a request for discovery (under Rule 71, 72, 73, or 74) or to a request for admission (under Rule 90) in a manner which was complete when made, is under no duty to supplement the response to include information thereafter acquired, except as follows:

(1) A party is under a duty seasonably to supplement the response with respect to any matter directly addressed to: (A) The identity and location of persons having knowledge of discoverable matters, and (B) the identity of each person expected to be called as an expert witness at trial, the subject matter on which such person is expected to testify, and the substance of such person's testimony. In respect of the requirement to furnish reports of expert wit- nesses, see Rule 143(g)(1).

(2) A party is under a duty seasonably to amend a prior response if the party obtains information upon the basis of which the party knows that: (A) The response was incor- rect when made, or (B) the response, though correct when made, is no longer true and the circumstances are such that a failure to amend the response is in substance a knowing concealment.

(3) A duty to supplement responses may be imposed by order of the Court, agreement of the parties, or at any time prior to trial through new requests for supplementation of prior responses.

RULE 103. PROTECTIVE ORDERS

[1](a) **Authorized Orders:** Upon motion by a party or any

other affected person, and for good cause shown, the Court may make any order which justice requires to protect a party or other person from annoyance, embarrassment, oppression, or undue burden or expense, including but not limited to one or more of the following:

(1)   That the particular method or procedure not be used.

(2)   That the method or procedure be used only on specified terms and conditions, including a designation of the time or place.

(3)   That a method or procedure be used other than the one selected by the party.

(4)   That certain matters not be inquired into, or that the method be limited to certain matters or to any other extent.

(5)   That the method or procedure be conducted with no one present except persons designated by the Court.

(6)   That a deposition or other written materials, after being sealed, be opened only by order of the Court.

(7)   That a trade secret or other information not be disclosed or be disclosed only in a designated way.

(8)   That the parties simultaneously file specified documents or information enclosed in sealed envelopes to be opened as directed by the Court.

(9)   That expense involved in a method or procedure be borne in a particular manner or by specified person or persons.

(10)   That documents or records (including electronically stored information) be impounded by the Court to ensure their availability for purpose of review by the parties prior to trial and use at the trial.

If a discovery request has been made, then the movant shall attach as an exhibit to a motion for a protective order under this Rule a copy of any discovery request in respect of which the motion is filed.

(b) Denials: If a motion for a protective order is denied in whole or in part, then the Court may, on such terms or conditions it deems just, order any party or person to comply or to respond in accordance with the procedure involved.

RULE 104. ENFORCEMENT ACTION AND SANCTIONS [1]

(a)   Failure To Attend Deposition or To Answer Interrogatories or Respond to Request for Inspection or Production: If a party, or an officer, director, or managing agent of a party, or a person designated in accordance with Rule 74(b) or (c) or Rule 81(c) to testify on behalf of a party fails: (1) To appear before the officer who is to take such person's deposition pursuant to Rule 74, 81, 82, 83, or 84; (2) to serve answers or objections to interrogatories submitted under Rule 71, after proper service thereof; or (3) to serve a written response to a request for production or inspection submitted under Rule 72 or 73 after proper service of the request, then the Court on motion may make such orders in regard to the failure as are just, and among others it may take any action authorized under paragraph (b) or (c) of this Rule. If any person, after being served with a subpoena or having waived such service, willfully fails to appear before the officer who is to take such person's deposition or refuses to be sworn, or if any person willfully fails to obey an order requiring such person to answer designated interrogatories or questions, then such failure may be considered contempt of court. The failure to act described in this paragraph (a) may not be excused on the ground that the deposition sought, the interrogatory submitted, or the production or inspection sought, is objectionable, unless the party failing to act has theretofore raised the objection, or has applied for a protective order under Rule 103, with respect thereto at the proper time and in the proper manner, and the Court has either sustained or granted or not yet ruled on the objection or the application for the order.

(b) Failure To Answer: If a person fails to answer a question or interrogatory propounded or submitted in accordance with Rule 71, 74, 81, 82, 83, or 84, or fails to respond to a request to produce or inspect or fails to produce or permit the inspection in accordance with Rule 72 or 73, or fails to make a designation in accordance with Rule 74(b) or (c) or Rule 81(c), the aggrieved party may, within the time for completion of discovery under Rule 70(a)(2), move the Court for an order compelling an answer, response, or compliance with the request, as the case may be. When taking a deposition on oral examination, the examination may be completed on other matters or the examination adjourned, as the proponent of the question may prefer, before applying for such order.

(c) Sanctions: If a party or an officer, director, or managing agent of a party or a person designated in accordance with Rule 74(b) or (c) or Rule 81(c) fails to obey an order made by the Court with respect to the provisions of Rule 71, 72, 73, 74, 81, 82, 83, 84, or 90, then the Court may make such orders as to the failure as are just, and among others the following:

(1) An order that the matter regarding which the order was made or any other designated facts shall be taken to be established for the purposes of the case in accordance with the claim of the party obtaining the order.

(2) An order refusing to allow the disobedient party to support or oppose designated claims or defenses, or prohibiting such party from introducing designated matters in evidence.

(3) An order striking out pleadings or parts thereof, staying further proceedings until the order is obeyed, dismissing the case or any part thereof, or rendering a judgment

by default against the disobedient party.

(4) In lieu of the foregoing orders or in addition thereto, the Court may treat as a contempt of the Court the failure to obey any such order, and the Court may also require the party failing to obey the order or counsel advising such party, or both, to pay the reasonable expenses, including counsel's fees, caused by the failure, unless the Court finds that the failure was substantially justified or that other circumstances make an award of expenses unjust.

(d) Evasive or Incomplete Answer or Response: For purposes of this Rule and Rules 71, 72, 73, 74, 81, 82, 83, 84, and 90, an evasive or incomplete answer or response is to be treated as a failure to answer or respond.

(e) Failure to Provide Electronically Stored Information: Absent exceptional circumstances, sanctions may not be imposed under this Rule on a party for failing to provide electronically stored information that was lost as a result of the routine, good-faith operation of an electronic information system.

TITLE XI PRETRIAL CONFERENCES

RULE 110. PRETRIAL CONFERENCES

(a) General: In appropriate cases, the Court will undertake to confer with the parties in pretrial conferences with a view to narrowing issues, stipulating facts, simplifying the presentation of evidence, or otherwise assisting in the preparation for trial or possible disposition of the case in whole or in part without trial.

(b) Cases Calendared: Either party in a case listed on any trial calendar may request of the Court, or the Court on its own motion may order, a pretrial conference. The Court may, in its discretion, set the case for a pretrial conference during the trial session. If sufficient reason appears therefor, a pretrial conference will be scheduled prior to the call of the calendar at such time and place as may be practicable and appropriate.

(c) Cases Not Calendared: If a case is not listed on a trial calendar, the Chief Judge, in the exercise of discretion, upon motion of either party or sua sponte, may list such case for a pretrial conference upon a calendar in the place requested for trial, or may assign the case for a pretrial conference either in Washington, D.C., or in any other convenient place.

(d) Conditions: A request or motion for a pretrial conference shall include a statement of the reasons therefor. Pretrial conferences will in no circumstances be held as a substitute for the conferences required between the parties in order to comply with the provisions of Rule 91, but a pretrial conference, for the purpose of assisting the parties in entering into the stipulations called for by Rule 91, will be held by the

Court where the party requesting such pretrial conference has in good faith attempted without success to obtain such stipulations from such party's adversary. Nor will any pretrial conference be held where the Court is satisfied that the request therefor is frivolous or is made for purposes of delay.

(e) Order: The Court may, in its discretion, issue appropriate pretrial orders.

TITLE XII

DECISION WITHOUT TRIAL

RULE 120. JUDGMENT ON THE PLEADINGS

(a) General: After the pleadings are closed but within such time as not to delay the trial, any party may move for judgment on the pleadings. The motion shall be filed and served in accordance with the requirements otherwise applicable. See Rules 50 and 54. Such motion shall be disposed of before trial unless the Court determines otherwise.

(b) Matters Outside Pleadings: If, on a motion for judgment on the pleadings, matters outside the pleadings are presented to and not excluded by the Court, the motion shall be treated as one for summary judgment and shall be dis- posed of as provided in Rule 121, and all parties shall be given reasonable opportunity to present all material made pertinent to such a motion by Rule 121.

RULE 121. SUMMARY JUDGMENT

[1]**(a) General:** Either party may move, with or without supporting affidavits or declarations, for a summary adjudication in the moving party's favor upon all or any part of the legal issues in controversy. Such motion may be made at any time commencing 30 days after the pleadings are closed but within such time as not to delay the trial, and in any event no later than 60 days before the first day of the Court's session at which the case is calendared for trial, unless otherwise permitted by the Court.

[2]**(b) Motion and Proceedings Thereon:** The motion shall be filed and served in accordance with the requirements otherwise applicable. See Rules 50 and 54. An opposing written response, with or without supporting affidavits or declarations, shall be filed within such period as the Court may direct. A decision shall thereafter be rendered if the pleadings, answers to interrogatories, depositions, admissions, and any other acceptable materials, together with the affidavits or declarations, if any, show that there is no genuine dispute as to any material fact and that a decision may be rendered as a matter of law. A partial summary adjudication may be made which does not dispose of all the issues in the case.

(c) Case Not Fully Adjudicated on Motion: If, on motion under this Rule, decision is not rendered upon the whole case or for all the relief asked and a trial is necessary, the Court may ascertain, by examining the pleadings and the evidence before it and by interrogating counsel, what material facts exist without substantial controversy and what material facts are actually and in good faith controverted. It may thereupon make an order specifying the facts that ap- pear to be without substantial controversy, including the ex- tent to which the relief sought is not in controversy, and di- recting such further proceedings in the case as are just. Upon the trial of the case, the facts so specified shall be deemed established, and the trial shall be concluded accordingly.

[1]**(d) Form of Affidavits or Declarations; Further Testimony; Defense Required:** Supporting and opposing affidavits or declarations shall be made on personal knowl- edge, shall set forth such facts as would be admissible in evi- dence, and shall show affirmatively that the affiant or declar- ant is competent to testify to the matters stated therein. Sworn or certified copies of all papers or parts thereof re- ferred to in an affidavit or a declaration shall be attached thereto or filed therewith. The Court may permit affidavits or declarations to be supplemented or opposed by answers to interrogatories, depositions, further affidavits or declarations, or other acceptable materials, to the extent that other appli- cable conditions in these Rules are satisfied for utilizing such procedures. When a motion for summary judgment is made and supported as provided in this Rule, an adverse party may not rest upon the mere allegations or denials of such party's pleading, but such party's response, by affidavits or declarations or as otherwise provided in this Rule, must set forth specific facts showing that there is a genuine dispute for trial. If the adverse party does not so respond, then a de- cision, if appropriate, may be entered against such party.

(e) When Affidavits or Declarations Are Unavailable: If it appears from the affidavits or declarations of a party opposing the motion that such party cannot for reasons stated present by affidavit or declaration facts essential to justify such party's opposition, then the Court may deny the motion or may order a continuance to permit affidavits or declarations to be obtained or other steps to be taken or may make such other order as is just. If it appears from the affidavits or declarations of a party opposing the motion that such party's only legally available method of contravening the facts set forth in the supporting affidavits or declarations of the moving party is through cross-examination of such affiants or declarants or the testimony of third parties from whom affidavits or declarations cannot be secured, then such a showing may be deemed sufficient to establish that the facts set forth in such supporting affidavits or declarations are genuinely disputed.

[2]**(f) Affidavits or Declarations Made in Bad Faith:** If it appears to the satisfaction of the Court at any time that any of

the affidavits or declarations presented pursuant to this Rule are presented in bad faith or for the purpose of delay, then the Court may order the party employing them to pay to the other party the amount of the reasonable expenses which the filing of the affidavits or declarations caused the other party to incur, including reasonable counsel's fees, and any offending party or counsel may be ad- judged guilty of contempt or otherwise disciplined by the Court.

RULE 122. SUBMISSION WITHOUT TRIAL

(a) General: Any case not requiring a trial for the submission of evidence (as, for example, where sufficient facts have been admitted, stipulated, established by deposition, or included in the record in some other way) may be submitted at any time after joinder of issue (see Rule 38) by motion of the parties filed with the Court. The parties need not wait for the case to be calendared for trial and need not appear in Court.

Burden of Proof: The fact of submission of a case, under paragraph (a) of this Rule, does not alter the burden of proof, or the requirements otherwise applicable with respect to adducing proof, or the effect of failure of proof.

RULE 123. DEFAULT AND DISMISSAL

(a) Default: If any party has failed to plead or otherwise proceed as provided by these Rules or as required by the Court, then such party may be held in default by the Court either on motion of another party or on the initiative of the Court. Thereafter, the Court may enter a decision against the defaulting party, upon such terms and conditions as the Court may deem proper, or may impose such sanctions (see, e.g., Rule 104) as the Court may deem appropriate. The Court may, in its discretion, conduct hearings to ascertain whether a default has been committed, to determine the decision to be entered or the sanctions to be imposed, or to ascertain the truth of any matter.

(b) Dismissal: For failure of a petitioner properly to prosecute or to comply with these Rules or any order of the Court or for other cause which the Court deems sufficient, the Court may dismiss a case at any time and enter a decision against the petitioner. The Court may, for similar reasons, decide against any party any issue as to which such party has the burden of proof, and such decision shall be treated as a dismissal for purposes of paragraphs (c) and (d) of this Rule.

(c) Setting Aside Default or Dismissal: For reasons deemed sufficient by the Court and upon motion expeditiously made, the Court may set aside a default or dismissal or the decision rendered thereon.

(d) Effect of Decision on Default or Dismissal: A decision rendered upon a default or in consequence of a dis- missal, other than a dismissal for lack of jurisdiction, shall operate as an adjudication on the merits.

RULE 124. ALTERNATIVE DISPUTE RESOLUTION [1]

(a) Voluntary Binding Arbitration: The parties may move that any factual issue in controversy be resolved through voluntary binding arbitration. Such a motion may be made at any time after a case is at issue and before trial. Upon the filing of such a motion, the Chief Judge will assign the case to a Judge or Special Trial Judge for disposition of the motion and supervision of any subsequent arbitration.

(1) *Stipulation Required:* The parties shall attach to any motion filed under paragraph (a) a stipulation executed by each party or counsel for each party. Such stipulation shall include the matters specified in subparagraph (2).

(2) *Content of Stipulation:* The stipulation required by subparagraph (1) shall include the following:

(A) A statement of the issues to be resolved by the arbitrator;

(B) an agreement by the parties to be bound by the findings of the arbitrator in respect of the issues to be resolved;

(C) the identity of the arbitrator or the procedure to be used to select the arbitrator;

(D) the manner in which payment of the arbitrator's compensation and expenses, as well as any related fees and costs, is to be allocated among the parties;

(E) a prohibition against ex parte communication with the arbitrator; and

(F) such other matters as the parties deem to be appropriate.

(3) *Order by Court:* The arbitrator will be appointed by order of the Court, which order may contain such directions to the arbitrator and to the parties as the Judge or Special Trial Judge considers to be appropriate.

(4) *Report by Parties:* The parties shall promptly report to the Court the findings made by the arbitrator and shall attach to their report any written report or summary that the arbitrator may have prepared.

(b) Voluntary Nonbinding Mediation: The parties may move by joint or unopposed motion that any issue incontroversy be resolved through voluntary nonbinding mediation. Such a motion may be made at any time after a case is at issue and before the decision in the case is final.

(1) *Order by Court:* The mediation shall proceed in accordance with an order of the Court setting forth such directions to the parties as the Court considers to be appro-

priate.

(2) *Tax Court Judge or Special Trial Judge as Mediator:* A Judge or Special Trial Judge of the Court may act as mediator in any case pending before the Court if:

(A) the motion makes a specific request that a Judge or Special Trial Judge be designated as such, and

(B) a Judge or Special Trial Judge is so designated by order of the Chief Judge.

(c) Other Methods of Dispute Resolution: Nothing contained in this Rule shall be construed to exclude use by the parties of other forms of voluntary disposition of cases.

TITLE XIII CALENDARS AND CONTINUANCES

RULE 130. MOTIONS AND OTHER MATTERS

[1]**(a) Calendars:** If a hearing is to be held on a motion or other matter, apart from a trial on the merits, then such hearing may be held on a motion calendar in Washington, D.C., unless the Court, on its own motion or on the motion of a party, shall direct otherwise. As to hearings at other places, see Rule 50(b)(2). The parties will be given notice of the place and time of hearing.

(b) Failure To Attend: The Court may hear a matter ex parte where a party fails to appear at such a hearing. With respect to attendance at such hearings, see Rule 50(c).

RULE 131. TRIAL CALENDARS

(a) General: Each case, when at issue, will be placed upon a calendar for trial in accordance with Rule 140. The Clerk shall notify the parties of the place and time for which the calendar is set.

(b) Standing Pretrial Order: In order to facilitate the orderly and efficient disposition of all cases on a trial calendar, at the direction of the trial judge, the Clerk shall include with the notice of trial a Standing Pretrial Order or other instructions for trial preparation. Unexcused failure to comply with any such order may subject a party or a party's counsel to sanctions. See, e.g., Rules 104, 123, and 202.

(c) Calendar Call: Each case appearing on a trial calendar will be called at the time and place scheduled. At the call, counsel or the parties shall indicate their estimate of the time required for trial. The cases for trial will thereupon be tried in due course, but not necessarily in the order listed.

RULE 132. SPECIAL OR OTHER CALENDARS

Special or other calendars may be scheduled by the Court, upon motion or at its own initiative, for any purpose which the Court may deem appropriate. The parties involved shall be notified of the place and time of such calendars.

RULE 133. CONTINUANCES

A case or matter scheduled on a calendar may be continued by the Court upon motion or at its own initiative. A motion for continuance shall inform the Court of the position of the other parties with respect thereto, either by endorsement thereon by the other parties or by a representation of the moving party. A motion for continuance based upon the pendency in a court of a related case or cases shall include the name and docket number of any such related case, the names of counsel for the parties in such case, and the status of such case, and shall identify all issues common to any such related case. Continuances will be granted only in exceptional circumstances. Conflicting engagements of counsel or employment of new counsel ordinarily will not be regarded as ground for continuance. A motion for continuance, filed 30 days or less prior to the date to which it is directed, may be set for hearing on that date, but ordinarily will be deemed dilatory and will be denied unless the ground therefor arose during that period or there was good reason for not making the motion sooner. As to extensions of time, see Rule 25(c).

TITLE XIV TRIALS

RULE 140. PLACE OF TRIAL

(a) Request for Place of Trial: The petitioner, at the time of filing the petition, shall file a request for place of trial showing the place at which the petitioner would prefer the trial to be held. If the petitioner has not filed such a re- quest, then the Commissioner, at the time the answer is filed, shall file a request showing the place of trial preferred by the Commissioner. The Court will make reasonable efforts to conduct the trial at the location most convenient to that requested where suitable facilities are available. The parties shall be notified of the place at which the trial will be held.

(b) Form: Such request shall be set forth on a paper separate from the petition or answer. See Form 5, Appendix I.

(c) Motion To Change Place of Trial: If a party de- sires a change in the place of trial, then such party shall file a motion to that effect, stating fully the reasons therefor. Such motions, made after the notice of the time of trial has been issued, may be deemed dilatory and may be denied un- less the ground therefor arose during that period or there was good reason for not making the motion sooner.

RULE 141. CONSOLIDATION; SEPARATE TRIALS

(a) Consolidation: When cases involving a common question of law or fact are pending before the Court, it may order a joint hearing or trial of any or all the matters in issue, it may order all the cases consolidated, and it may make such orders concerning proceedings therein as may tend to avoid unnecessary costs, delay, or duplication. Simi- lar action may be taken where cases involve different tax li- abilities of the same parties, notwithstanding the absence of a common issue. Unless otherwise permitted by the Court for good cause shown, a motion to consolidate cases may be filed only after all the cases sought to be consolidated have be- come at issue. The caption of a motion to consolidate shall include all of the names and docket numbers of the cases sought to be consolidated arranged in chronological order (i.e., the oldest case first). Unless otherwise ordered, the caption of all documents subsequently filed in consolidated cases shall include all of the docket numbers arranged in chrono- logical order, but may include only the name of the oldest case with an appropriate indication of other parties.

(b) Separate Trials: The Court, in furtherance of con- venience or to avoid prejudice, or when separate trials will be conducive to expedition or economy, may order a separate trial of any one or more claims, defenses, or issues, or of the tax liability of any party or parties. The Court may enter ap- propriate orders or decisions with respect to any such claims, defenses, issues, or parties that are tried separately. As to severance of parties or claims, see Rule 61(b).

RULE 142. BURDEN OF PROOF

(a) General: (1) The burden of proof shall be upon the petitioner, except as otherwise provided by statute or deter- mined by the Court; and except that, in respect of any new matter, increases in deficiency, and affirmative defenses, pleaded in the answer, it shall be upon the respondent. As to affirmative defenses, see Rule 39.

(2) See Code section 7491 where credible evidence is in- troduced by the taxpayer, or any item of income is recon- structed by the Commissioner solely through the use of statistical information on unrelated taxpayers, or any pen- alty, addition to tax, or additional amount is determined by the Commissioner.

(b) Fraud: In any case involving the issue of fraud with intent to evade tax, the burden of proof in respect of that issue is on the respondent, and that burden of proof is to be carried by clear and convincing evidence. See Code sec. 7454(a).

(c) Foundation Managers; Trustees; Organization Managers: In any case involving the issue of the knowing conduct of a foundation manager as set forth in the provi- sions of Code section 4941, 4944, or 4945, or the knowing conduct of a trustee as set forth in the provisions of Code sec- tion 4951 or 4952, or the knowing conduct of an organization manager as set forth in the provisions of Code section 4912 or 4955, the burden of proof in respect of such issue is on the respondent, and such burden of proof is to be carried by clear and convincing evidence. See Code sec. 7454(b).

(d) Transferee Liability: The burden of proof is on the respondent to show that a petitioner is liable as a transferee of property of a taxpayer, but not to show that the taxpayer was liable for the tax. See Code sec. 6902(a).

(e) Accumulated Earnings Tax: Where the notice of deficiency is based in whole or in part on an allegation of accumulation of corporate earnings and profits beyond the reasonable needs of the business, the burden of proof with respect to such allegation is determined in accordance with Code section 534. If the petitioner has submitted to the respondent a statement which is claimed to satisfy the requirements of Code section 534(c), the Court will ordinarily, on timely motion filed after the case has been calendared for trial, rule prior to the trial on whether such statement is sufficient to shift the burden of proof to the respondent to the limited extent set forth in Code section 534(a)(2).

RULE 143. EVIDENCE [1]

(a) General: Trials before the Court will be conducted in accordance with the rules of evidence applicable in trials without a jury in the United States District Court for the District of Columbia. See Code sec. 7453. To the extent applicable to such trials, those rules include the rules of evidence in the Federal Rules of Civil Procedure and any rules of evidence generally applicable in the Federal courts (including the United States District Court for the District of Columbia). Evidence which is relevant only to the issue of a party's entitlement to reasonable litigation or administrative costs shall not be introduced during the trial of the case (other than a case commenced under Title XXVI of these Rules, relating to actions for administrative costs). As to claims for reasonable litigation or administrative costs and their dis- position, see Rules 231 and 232. As to evidence in an action for administrative costs, see Rule 274 (and that Rule's incorporation of the provisions of Rule 174(b)).

(b) Testimony: The testimony of a witness generally must be taken in open court except as otherwise provided by the Court or these Rules. For good cause in compelling circumstances and with appropriate safeguards, the Court may permit testimony in open court by contemporaneous transmission from a different location.

[1]**(c) Ex Parte Statements:** Ex parte affidavits or declarations, statements in briefs, and unadmitted allegations in pleadings do not constitute evidence. As to allegations in pleadings not denied, see Rules 36(c) and 37(c) and (d).

82

(d) Depositions: Testimony taken by deposition shall not be treated as evidence in a case until offered and received in evidence. Error in the transcript of a deposition may be corrected by agreement of the parties, or by the Court on proof it deems satisfactory to show an error exists and the correction to be made, subject to the requirements of Rules 81(h)(1) and 85(e). As to the use of a deposition, see Rule 81(i).

(e) Documentary Evidence: (1) *Copies:* A copy is admissible to the same extent as an original unless a genuine question is raised as to the authenticity of the original or in the circumstances it would be unfair to admit the copy in lieu of the original. Where the original is admitted in evidence, a clearly legible copy may be substituted later for the original or such part thereof as may be material or relevant, upon leave granted in the discretion of the Court.

(2) *Return of Exhibits:* Exhibits may be disposed of as the Court deems advisable. A party desiring the return at such party's expense of any exhibit belonging to such party, shall, within 90 days after the decision of the case by the Court has become final, make written application to the Clerk, suggesting a practical manner of delivery. If such application is not timely made, the exhibits in the case will be destroyed.

(f) Interpreters: The parties ordinarily will be expected to make their own arrangements for obtaining and compensating interpreters. However, the Court may appoint an interpreter of its own selection and may fix the interpreter's reasonable compensation, which compensation shall be paid by one or more of the parties or otherwise as the Court may direct.

[1]**(g) Expert Witness Reports:** (1) Unless otherwise permitted by the Court upon timely request, any party who calls an expert witness shall cause that witness to prepare a written report for submission to the Court and to the op- posing party if the witness is one retained or specially employed to provide expert testimony in the case or one whose duties as the party's employee regularly involve giving expert testimony. The report, prepared and signed by the witness, shall contain:

(A) a complete statement of all opinions the witness expresses and the basis and reasons for them;

(B) the facts or data considered by the witness in forming them;

(C) any exhibits used to summarize or support them;

(D) the witness's qualifications, including a list of all publications authored in the previous 10 years;

(E) a list of all other cases in which, during the previous 4 years, the witness testified as an expert at trial or by deposition; and

(F) a statement of the compensation to be paid for the study and testimony in the case.

(2) The report will be marked as an exhibit, identified by the witness, and received in evidence as the direct testimony of the expert witness, unless the Court determines that the witness is not qualified as an expert. Additional direct testimony with respect to the report may be allowed to clarify or emphasize matters in the report, to cover matters arising after the preparation of the report, or otherwise at the discretion of the Court. After the case is calendared for trial or assigned to a Judge or Special Trial Judge, each party who calls any expert witness shall serve on each other party, and shall submit to the Court, not later than 30 days before the call of the trial calendar on which the case shall appear, a copy of all expert witness reports prepared pursuant to this subparagraph. An expert witness's testimony will be excluded altogether for failure to comply with the provisions of this paragraph, unless the failure is shown to be due to good cause and unless the failure does not unduly prejudice the opposing party, such as by significantly impairing the opposing party's ability to cross-examine the expert witness or by denying the opposing party the reasonable opportunity to obtain evidence in rebuttal to the expert witness's testimony.

(3) The Court ordinarily will not grant a request to permit an expert witness to testify without a written report where the expert witness's testimony is based on third- party contacts, comparable sales, statistical data, or other detailed, technical information. The Court may grant such a request, for example, where the expert witness testifies only with respect to industry practice or only in rebuttal to another expert witness.

(4) For circumstances under which the transcript of the deposition of an expert witness may serve as the written report required by subparagraph (1), see Rule 74(d).

RULE 144. EXCEPTIONS UNNECESSARY

Formal exceptions to rulings or orders of the Court are unnecessary. It is sufficient that a party at the time the ruling or order of the Court is made or sought, makes known to the Court the action which such party desires the Court to take or such party's objection to the action of the Court and the grounds therefor; and, if a party has no opportunity to object to a ruling or order at the time it is made, the absence of an objection does not thereafter prejudice such party.

RULE 145. EXCLUSION OF PROPOSED WITNESSES

(a) **Exclusion:** At the request of a party, the Court shall order witnesses excluded so that they cannot hear the testimony of other witnesses and it may make the order on its own motion. This Rule does not authorize exclusion of: (1)

A party who is a natural person, or (2) an officer or employee of a party which is not a natural person designated as its representative by its attorney, or (3) a person whose presence is shown by a party to be essential to the presentation of such party's cause.

(b) Contempt: Among other measures which the Court may take in the circumstances, it may punish as for a contempt: (1) Any witness who remains within hearing of the proceedings after such exclusion has been directed, that fact being noted in the record; and (2) any person (witness, counsel, or party) who willfully violates instructions issued by the Court with respect to such exclusion.

RULE 146. DETERMINATION OF FOREIGN LAW

A party who intends to raise an issue concerning the law of a foreign country shall give notice in the pleadings or other reasonable written notice. The Court, in determining foreign law, may consider any relevant material or source, including testimony, whether or not submitted by a party or otherwise admissible. The Court's determination shall be treated as a ruling on a question of law.

RULE 147. SUBPOENAS [1]

(a) Attendance of Witnesses; Form; Issuance: Every subpoena shall be issued under the seal of the Court, shall state the name of the Court and the caption of the case, and shall command each person to whom it is directed to attend and give testimony at a time and place therein specified. A subpoena, including a subpoena for the production of documentary evidence or electronically stored information, signed and sealed but otherwise blank, shall be issued to a party requesting it, who shall fill it in before service. Subpoenas may be obtained at the Office of the Clerk in Washington, D.C., or from a trial clerk at a trial session. See Code sec. 7456(a).

(b) Production of Documentary Evidence and Electronically Stored Information: A subpoena may also command the person to whom it is directed to produce the books, papers, documents, electronically stored information, or tangible things designated therein, and may specify the form or forms in which electronically stored information is to be produced. The Court, upon motion made promptly and in any event at or before the time specified in the subpoena for compliance therewith, may (1) quash or modify the subpoena if it is unreasonable and oppressive, or (2) condition denial   of the motion upon the advancement by the person in whose behalf the subpoena is issued of the reasonable cost of pro- ducing the books, papers, documents, electronically stored in- formation, or tangible things.

(c) Service: A subpoena may be served by a United States marshal, or by a deputy marshal, or by any other per- son who is not a party and is not less than 18 years of age. Service of a subpoena upon a person named therein shall be made by delivering a copy thereof to such person and by tendering to such person the fees for one day's attendance and the mileage allowed by law. When the subpoena is issued on behalf of the Commissioner, fees and mileage need not be tendered. See Rule 148 for fees and mileage payable. The person making service of a subpoena shall make the return thereon in accordance with the form appearing in the subpoena.

(d) Subpoena for Taking Depositions: (1) *Issuance and Response:* The order of the Court approving the taking of a deposition pursuant to Rule 81(b)(2), the executed stipulation pursuant to Rule 81(d), or the service of the notice of deposition pursuant to Rule 74(b)(2) or (c)(2), constitutes authorization for issuance of subpoenas for the persons named or described therein. The subpoena may command the person to whom it is directed to produce and permit inspection and copying of designated books, papers, documents, electronically stored information, or tangible things, which come with- in the scope of the order or stipulation pursuant to which the deposition is taken. Within 15 days after service of the subpoena or such earlier time designated therein for compliance, the person to whom the subpoena is directed may serve upon the party on whose behalf the subpoena has been issued written objections to compliance with the subpoena in any or all respects. Such objections should not include objections made, or which might have been made, to the application to take the deposition pursuant to Rule 81(b)(2) or to the notice of deposition under Rule 74(b)(2) or (c)(2). If an objection is made, the party serving the subpoena shall not be entitled to compliance therewith to the extent of such objection, except as the Court may order otherwise upon application to it. Such application for an order may be made, with notice to the other party and to any other objecting persons, at any time before or during the taking of the deposition, subject to the time requirements of Rule 70(a)(2) or 81(b)(2). As to availability of protective orders, see Rule 103; and, as to enforcement of such subpoenas, see Rule 104.

(2) *Place of Examination:* The place designated in the subpoena for examination of the deponent shall be the place specified in the notice of deposition served pursuant to Rule 74(b)(2) or (c)(2), in a motion to take deposition under Rule 74(c)(3) or (4), in the order of the Court referred to in Rule 81(b)(2), or in the executed stipulation referred to in Rule 81(d). With respect to a deposition to be taken in a foreign country, see Rules 74(e)(2), 81(e)(2), and 84(a).

(e) Contempt: Failure by any person without adequate excuse to obey a subpoena served upon any such person may be deemed a contempt of the Court.

RULE 148. FEES AND MILEAGE

(a) **Amount:** Any witness summoned to a hearing or trial, or whose deposition is taken, shall receive the same fees and mileage as witnesses in the United States District Courts. With respect to fees and mileage paid to witnesses in the United States District Court, see 28 U.S.C. section 1821.

(b) **Tender:** No witness, other than one for the Commissioner, shall be required to testify until the witness shall have been tendered the fees and mileage to which the witness is entitled according to law. With respect to witnesses for the Commissioner, see Code section 7457(b)(1).

(c) **Payment:** The party at whose instance a witness appears shall be responsible for the payment of the fees and mileage to which that witness is entitled.

RULE 149. FAILURE TO APPEAR OR TO ADDUCE EVIDENCE

(a) **Attendance at Trials:** The unexcused absence of a party or a party's counsel when a case is called for trial will not be ground for delay. The case may be dismissed for failure properly to prosecute, or the trial may proceed and the case be regarded as submitted on the part of the absent party or parties.

(b) **Failure of Proof:** Failure to produce evidence, in support of an issue of fact as to which a party has the burden of proof and which has not been conceded by such party's adversary, may be ground for dismissal or for determination of the affected issue against that party. Facts may be established by stipulation in accordance with Rule 91, but the mere filing of such stipulation does not relieve the party, upon whom rests the burden of proof, of the necessity of properly producing evidence in support of facts not adequately established by such stipulation. As to submission of a case without trial, see Rule 122.

RULE 150. RECORD OF PROCEEDINGS

[1](a) **General:** Hearings and trials before the Court shall be recorded or otherwise reported, and a transcript thereof shall be made if, in the opinion of the Court or the Judge or Special Trial Judge presiding at a hearing or trial, a permanent record is deemed appropriate. Transcripts shall be supplied to the parties and other persons at such charges as may be fixed or approved by the Court.

(b) **Transcript as Evidence:** Whenever the testimony of a witness at a trial or hearing which was recorded or otherwise reported is admissible in evidence at a later trial or hearing, it may be proved by the transcript thereof duly certified by the person who reported the testimony.

RULE 151. BRIEFS

[2](a) **General:** Briefs shall be filed after trial or submission of a case, except as otherwise directed by the presiding Judge or Special Trial Judge. In addition to or in lieu of briefs, the presiding Judge or Special Trial Judge may permit or direct the parties to make oral argument or file memoranda or statements of authorities. The Court may return without filing any brief that does not conform to the requirements of this Rule.

[3](b) **Time for Filing Briefs:** Briefs may be filed simultaneously or seriatim, as the presiding Judge or Special Trial Judge directs. The following times for filing briefs shall prevail in the absence of any different direction by the presiding Judge or Special Trial Judge:

(1) *Simultaneous Briefs:* Opening briefs within 75 days after the conclusion of the trial, and answering briefs 45 days thereafter.

(2) *Seriatim Briefs:* Opening brief within 75 days after the conclusion of the trial, answering brief within 45 days thereafter, and reply brief within 30 days after the due date of the answering brief.

A party who fails to file an opening brief is not permitted to file an answering or reply brief except on leave granted by the Court. A motion for extension of time for filing any brief shall be made prior to the due date and shall recite that the moving party has advised such party's adversary and whether or not such adversary objects to the motion. As to the effect of extensions of time, see Rule 25(c).

[1](c) **Service:** Each brief shall be served upon the opposite party when it is filed, except that, in the event of simultaneous briefs, such brief shall be served by the Clerk after the corresponding brief of the other party has been filed, un- less the Court directs otherwise. Delinquent briefs will not be accepted unless accompanied by a motion setting forth reasons deemed sufficient by the Court to account for the delay. In the case of simultaneous briefs, the Court may return without filing a delinquent brief from a party after such party's adversary's brief has been served upon such party.

(d) **Number of Copies:** A signed original and two copies of each brief, plus an additional copy for each person to be served, shall be filed.

(e) **Form and Content:** All briefs shall conform to the requirements of Rule 23 and shall contain the following in the order indicated:

(1) On the first page, a table of contents with page references, followed by a list of all citations arranged alphabetically as to cited cases and stating the pages in the brief

at which cited. Citations shall be in italics when printed and underscored when typewritten.

(2) A statement of the nature of the controversy, the tax involved, and the issues to be decided.

(3) Proposed findings of fact (in the opening brief or briefs), based on the evidence, in the form of numbered statements, each of which shall be complete and shall consist of a concise statement of essential fact and not a recital of testimony nor a discussion or argument relating to the evidence or the law. In each such numbered statement, there shall be inserted references to the pages of the transcript or the exhibits or other sources relied upon to sup- port the statement. In an answering or reply brief, the party shall set forth any objections, together with the rea- sons therefor, to any proposed findings of any other party, showing the numbers of the statements to which the objections are directed; in addition, the party may set forth alternative proposed findings of fact.

(4) A concise statement of the points on which the party relies.

(5) The argument, which sets forth and discusses the points of law involved and any disputed questions of fact.

(6) The signature of counsel or the party submitting the brief. As to signature, see Rule 23(a)(3).

RULE 152. ORAL FINDINGS OF FACT OR OPINION

(a) General: Except in actions for declaratory judgment or for disclosure (see Titles XXI and XXII), the Judge, or the Special Trial Judge in any case in which the Special Trial Judge is authorized to make the decision of the Court pursuant to Code section 7436(c) or 7443A(b)(2), (3), (4), or (5), and (c), may, in the exercise of discretion, orally state the findings of fact or opinion if the Judge or Special Trial Judge is satisfied as to the factual conclusions to be reached in the case and that the law to be applied thereto is clear.

(b) Transcript: Oral findings of fact or opinion shall be recorded in the transcript of the hearing or trial. The pages of the transcript that contain such findings of fact or opinion (or a written summary thereof) shall be served by the Clerk upon all parties.

(c) Nonprecedential Effect: Opinions stated orally in accordance with paragraph (a) of this Rule shall not be relied upon as precedent, except as may be relevant for purposes of establishing the law of the case, res judicata, collateral estoppel, or other similar doctrine.

TITLE XV DECISION

RULE 155. COMPUTATION BY PARTIES FOR ENTRY OF DECISION

[1](a) **Agreed Computations:** Where the Court has filed or stated its opinion or issued a dispositive order determining the issues in a case, it may withhold entry of its decision for the purpose of permitting the parties to submit computations pursuant to the Court's determination of the issues, showing the correct amount to be included in the decision. Unless otherwise directed by the Court, if the parties are in agreement as to the amount to be included in the decision pursuant to the findings and conclusions of the Court, then they, or either of them, shall file with the Court within 90 days of service of the opinion or order an original and one copy of a computation showing the amount and that there is no disagreement that the figures shown are in accordance with the findings and conclusions of the Court. In the case of an overpayment, the computation shall also include the amount and date of each payment made by the petitioner. The Court will then enter its decision.

[2](b) **Procedure in Absence of Agreement:** If the parties are not in agreement as to the amount to be included in the decision in accordance with the findings and conclusions of the Court, then each party shall file with the Court a computation of the amount believed by such party to be in accordance with the Court's findings and conclusions. In the case of an overpayment, the computation shall also include the amount and date of each payment made by the petitioner. A party shall file such party's computation within 90 days of service of the opinion or order, unless otherwise directed by the Court. The Clerk will serve upon the opposite party a notice of such filing and if, on or before a date specified in the Clerk's notice, the opposite party fails to file an objection or an alternative computation, then the Court may enter decision in accordance with the computation already submitted. If in accordance with this Rule computations are submitted by the parties which differ as to the amount to be entered as the decision of the Court, then the parties may, at the Court's discretion, be afforded an opportunity to be heard in argument thereon and the Court will determine the correct amount and will enter its decision accordingly.

(c) **Limit on Argument:** Any argument under this Rule will be confined strictly to consideration of the correct computation of the amount to be included in the decision resulting from the findings and conclusions made by the Court, and no argument will be heard upon or consideration given to the issues or matters disposed of by the Court's findings and conclusions or to any new issues. This Rule is not to be regarded as affording an opportunity for retrial or reconsideration.

RULE 156. ESTATE TAX DEDUCTION DEVELOPING AT OR AFTER TRIAL

If the parties in an estate tax case are unable to agree under Rule 155, or under a remand, upon a deduction involving expenses incurred at or after the trial, then any party may move to reopen the case for further trial on that issue.

RULE 157. MOTION TO RETAIN FILE IN ESTATE TAX CASE INVOLVING SECTION 6166 ELECTION

In any estate tax case in which the time for payment of an amount of tax imposed by Code section 2001 has been extended under Code section 6166, the petitioner shall, after the decision is entered but before it becomes final, move the Court to retain the Court's official case file pending the commencement of any supplemental proceeding under Rule 262.

TITLE XVI

POSTTRIAL PROCEEDINGS

RULE 160. HARMLESS ERROR

No error in either the admission or the exclusion of evidence, and no error or defect in any ruling or order or in anything done or omitted by the Court or by any of the parties, is ground for granting a new trial or for vacating, modifying, or otherwise disturbing a decision or order, unless refusal to take such action appears to the Court inconsistent with substantial justice. The Court at every stage of a case will dis- regard any error or defect which does not affect the substan- tial rights of the parties.

RULE 161. MOTION FOR RECONSIDERATION OF FINDINGS OR OPINION

Any motion for reconsideration of an opinion or findings of fact, with or without a new or further trial, shall be filed within 30 days after a written opinion or the pages of the transcript that contain findings of fact or opinion stated oral- ly pursuant to Rule 152 (or a written summary thereof) have been served, unless the Court shall otherwise permit.

RULE 162. MOTION TO VACATE OR REVISE DECISION

Any motion to vacate or revise a decision, with or without a new or further trial, shall be filed within 30 days after the decision has been entered, unless the Court shall otherwise permit.

RULE 163. NO JOINDER OF MOTIONS UNDER RULES 161 AND 162

Motions under Rules 161 and 162 shall be made separately from each other and not joined to or made part of any other motion.

TITLE XVII SMALL TAX CASES[1]

RULE 170. GENERAL

The Rules of this Title XVII, referred to herein as the "Small Tax Case Rules", set forth the special provisions which are to be applied to small tax cases. The term "small tax case" means a case in which the amount in dispute is $50,000 or less (within the meaning of the Internal Revenue Code) and the Court has concurred in the petitioner's elec- tion. See Code secs. 7436(c), 7463. Except as otherwise pro- vided in these Small Tax Case Rules, the other Rules of prac- tice of the Court are applicable to such cases.

RULE 171. ELECTION OF SMALL TAX CASE PROCEDURE

With respect to classification of a case as a small tax case, the following shall apply:

(a) A petitioner who wishes to have the proceedings in the case conducted as a small tax case may so request at the time the petition is filed. See Rule 173.

[2]**(b)** If the Commissioner opposes the petitioner's request to have the proceedings conducted as a small tax case, then the Commissioner shall file with the answer a motion that the proceedings not be conducted as a small tax case.

[3]**(c)** A petitioner may, at any time after the petition is filed and before the trial commences, request that the proceedings be conducted as a small tax case. If such request is made after the answer is filed, then the Commissioner may move without leave of the Court that the proceedings not be conducted as a small tax case.

[4]**(d)** If such request is made in accordance with the provi- sions of this Rule 171, then the case will be docketed as a small tax case. The Court, on its own motion or on the motion of a party to the case, may, at any time before the trial commences, issue an order directing that the small tax case designation be removed and that the proceedings not be con- ducted as a small tax case. If no such order is issued, then the petitioner will be considered to have exercised the petitioner's option and the Court shall be deemed to have concurred therein.

RULE 172. REPRESENTATION

A petitioner in a small tax case may appear without representation or may be represented by any person admitted to practice before the Court. As to representation, see Rule 24.

RULE 173. PLEADINGS

(a) Petition: (1) *Form and Content:* The petition in a small tax case shall be substantially in accordance with Form 2 shown in Appendix I.

[1](2) *Filing Fee:* The fee for filing a petition shall be $60, payable at the time of filing. The payment of any fee under this paragraph may be waived if the petitioner establishes to the satisfaction of the Court by an affidavit or a declaration containing specific financial information the inability to make such payment.

(b) Answer: The Commissioner shall file an answer or shall move with respect to the petition within the periods specified in, and in accordance with the provisions of, Rule 36.

(c) Reply: A reply to the answer shall not be filed unless the Court otherwise directs. Any reply shall conform to the requirements of Rule 37(b). In the absence of a requirement of a reply, the provisions of the second sentence of Rule 37(c) shall not apply and the affirmative allegations of the answer shall be deemed denied.

RULE 174. TRIAL

(a) Place of Trial: At the time of filing the petition, the petitioner may, in accordance with Form 5 in Appendix I or by other separate writing, request the place where the petitioner would prefer the trial to be held. If the petitioner hasnot filed such a request, then the Commissioner, at the time the answer is filed, shall file a request showing the place of trial preferred by the Commissioner. The Court will make reasonable efforts to conduct the trial at the location most convenient to that requested where suitable facilities are available.

(b) Conduct of Trial and Evidence: Trials of small tax cases will be conducted as informally as possible consistent with orderly procedure, and any evidence deemed by the Court to have probative value shall be admissible.

(c) Briefs: Neither briefs nor oral arguments will be required in small tax cases unless the Court otherwise directs.

TITLE XVIII SPECIAL TRIAL JUDGES

RULE 180. ASSIGNMENT

The Chief Judge may from time to time designate a Special Trial Judge (see Rule 3(d)) to deal with any matter pending before the Court in accordance with these Rules and such directions as may be prescribed by the Chief Judge.

RULE 181. POWERS AND DUTIES[1]

Subject to the specifications and limitations in orders designating Special Trial Judges and in accordance with the applicable provisions of these Rules, Special Trial Judges have and shall exercise the power to regulate all proceedings in any matter before them, including the conduct of trials, pre- trial conferences, and hearings on motions, and to do all acts and take all measures necessary or proper for the efficient performance of their duties. They may require the production before them of evidence upon all matters embraced within their assignment, including the production of all books, papers, vouchers, documents, electronically stored information, and writings applicable thereto, and they have the authority to put witnesses on oath and to examine them. Special Trial Judges may rule upon the admissibility of evidence, in accordance with the provisions of Code sections 7453 and 7463, and may exercise such further and incidental authority, including ordering the issuance of subpoenas, as may be necessary for the conduct of trials or other proceedings.

RULE 182. CASES IN WHICH THE SPECIAL TRIAL JUDGE IS AUTHORIZED TO MAKE THE DECISION

Except as otherwise directed by the Chief Judge, the following procedure shall be observed in small tax cases (as defined in Rule 170); in cases where neither the amount of the deficiency placed in dispute (within the meaning of Code section 7463), nor the amount of any claimed overpayment, exceeds $50,000; in declaratory judgment actions; in lien and levy actions; and in whistleblower actions:

(a) Small Tax Cases: Except in cases where findings of fact or opinion are stated orally pursuant to Rule 152, a Special Trial Judge who conducts the trial of a small tax case shall, as soon after such trial as shall be practicable, prepare a summary of the facts and reasons for the proposed disposition of the case, which then shall be submitted promptly to the Chief Judge, or, if the Chief Judge shall so direct, to a Judge or Division of the Court.

(b) Cases Involving $50,000 or Less: Except in cases where findings of fact or opinion are stated orally pursuant to Rule 152, a Special Trial Judge who conducts the trial of a case (other than a small tax case) where neither the amount of the deficiency placed in dispute (within the meaning of Code section 7463), nor the amount of any claimed overpayment, exceeds $50,000 shall, as soon after such trial as shall be practicable, prepare proposed findings of fact and opinion, which shall then be submitted promptly to the Chief Judge.

94

(c) Declaratory Judgment, Lien and Levy, and Whistleblower Actions: A Special Trial Judge who conducts the trial of a declaratory judgment action or, except in cases where findings of fact or opinion are stated orally pursuant to Rule 152, a lien or levy or a whistleblower action, or to whom such a case is submitted for decision, shall, as soon after such trial or submission as shall be practicable, prepare proposed findings of fact and opinion, which shall then be submitted promptly to the Chief Judge.

(d) Decision: The Chief Judge may authorize the Special Trial Judge to make the decision of the Court in any small tax case (as defined in Rule 170); in any case where neither the amount of the deficiency placed in dispute (with- in the meaning of Code section 7463), nor the amount of any claimed overpayment, exceeds $50,000; in any declaratory judgment action; in any lien or levy action; and in any whistleblower action, subject to such conditions and review as the Chief Judge may provide.

(e) Procedure in Event of Assignment to a Judge: In the event the Chief Judge assigns a case (other than a small tax case) to a Judge to prepare a report in accordance with Code section 7460 and to make the decision of the Court, the proposed findings of fact and opinion previously submitted to the Chief Judge shall be filed as the Special

RULE 183. OTHER CASES

Except in cases subject to the provisions of Rule 182 or as otherwise provided, the following procedure shall be observed in cases tried before a Special Trial Judge:

(a) Trial and Briefs: A Special Trial Judge shall con- duct the trial of any assigned case. After such trial, the par- ties shall submit their briefs in accordance with the provisions of Rule 151. Unless otherwise directed, no further briefs shall be filed.

(b) Special Trial Judge's Recommendations: After all the briefs have been filed by all the parties or the time for doing so has expired, the Special Trial Judge shall file recommended findings of fact and conclusions of law and a copy of the recommended findings of fact and conclusions of law shall be served in accordance with Rule 21.

(c) Objections: Within 45 days after the service of the recommended findings of fact and conclusions of law, a party may serve and file specific, written objections to the recommended findings of fact and conclusions of law. A party may respond to another party's objections within 30 days after being served with a copy thereof. The above time periods may be extended by the Special Trial Judge. After the time for objections and responses has passed, the Chief Judge shall assign the case to a Judge for preparation of a report in accordance with Code section 7460. Unless a party shall have proposed a particular finding of fact, or unless the party shall have objected to another party's proposed finding of fact, the Judge may refuse to consider the party's objection to the Special Trial Judge's recommended findings of fact and conclusions of law for failure to make such a finding or for inclusion of such finding proposed by the other party, as the case may be.

(d) Action on the Recommendations: The Judge to whom the case is assigned may adopt the Special Trial Judge's recommended findings of fact and conclusions of law, or may modify or reject them in whole or in part, or may direct the filing of additional briefs, or may receive further evidence, or may direct oral argument, or may recommit there commended findings of fact and conclusions of law with instructions. The Judge's action on the Special Trial Judge's recommended findings of fact and conclusions of law shall be reflected in the record by an appropriate order or report. Due regard shall be given to the circumstance that the Special Trial Judge had the opportunity to evaluate the credibility of witnesses, and the findings of fact recommended by the Special Trial Judge shall be presumed to be correct.

TITLE XIX APPEALS

RULE 190. HOW APPEAL TAKEN

(a) General: Review of a decision of the Court by a United States Court of Appeals is obtained by filing a notice of appeal and the required filing fee with the Clerk of the Tax Court within 90 days after the decision is entered. If a timely notice of appeal is filed by one party, then any other party may take an appeal by filing a notice of appeal within 120 days after the Court's decision is entered. Code sec. 7483. For other requirements governing such an appeal, see rules 13 and 14 of the Federal Rules of Appellate Procedure. A suggested form of the notice of appeal is contained in Form 17 in Appendix I. See Code sec. 7482(a).

(b) Dispositive Orders: (1) *Entry and Appeal:* A dispositive order, including: (A) An order granting or denying a motion to restrain assessment or collection, made pursuant to Code section 6213(a), and (B) an order granting or denying a motion for review of a proposed sale of seized property, made pursuant to Code section 6863(b)(3)(C), shall be entered upon the record of the Court and served forthwith by the Clerk. Such an order shall be treated as a decision of the Court for purposes of appeal.

(2) *Stay of Proceedings:* Unless so ordered, proceedings in the Tax Court shall not be stayed by virtue of any order entered under Code section 6213(a) that is or may be the subject of an appeal pursuant to Code section 7482(a)(3) or any order entered under Code section 6863(b)(3)(C) that is or may be the subject of an appeal.

(c) Venue: For the circuit of the Court of Appeals to which the appeal is to be taken, see Code section 7482(b).

(d) Interlocutory Orders: For provisions governing appeals from interlocutory orders, see Rule 193.

RULE 191. PREPARATION OF THE RECORD ON APPEAL

The Clerk will prepare the record on appeal and forward it to the Clerk of the Court of Appeals pursuant to the notice of appeal filed with the Court, in accordance with rules 10 and 11 of the Federal Rules of Appellate Procedure. In addition, at the time the Clerk forwards the record on appeal to the Clerk of the Court of Appeals, the Clerk shall forward to each of the parties a copy of the index to the record on ap- peal.

RULE 192. BOND TO STAY ASSESSMENT AND COLLECTION

The filing of a notice of appeal does not stay assessment or collection of a deficiency redetermined by the Court un- less, on or before the filing of the notice of appeal, a bond is filed with the Court in accordance with Code section 7485.

RULE 193. APPEALS FROM INTERLOCUTORY ORDERS

(a) General: For the purpose of seeking the review of any order of the Tax Court which is not otherwise immediately appealable, a party may request the Court to include, or the Court on its own motion may include, a statement in such order that a controlling question of law is involved with respect to which there is a substantial ground for difference of opinion and that an immediate appeal from that order may materially advance the ultimate termination of the litigation. Any such request by a party shall be made by motion which shall set forth with particularity the grounds therefor and note whether there is any objection thereto. Any order by a Judge or Special Trial Judge of the Tax Court which includes the above statement shall be entered upon the records of the Court and served forthwith by the Clerk. See Code sec. 7482(a)(2). For appeals from interlocutory orders generally, see rules 5 and 14 of the Federal Rules of Appellate Procedure.

(b) Venue: For the circuit of the Court of Appeals to which an appeal from an interlocutory order may be taken, see Code section 7482(a)(2)(B) and (b).

(c) Stay of Proceedings: Unless so ordered, pro- ceedings in the Tax Court shall not be stayed by virtue of any interlocutory order that is or may be the subject of an appeal. See Code sec. 7482(a)(2)(A).

TITLE XX PRACTICE BEFORE THE COURT

RULE 200. ADMISSION TO PRACTICE AND PERIODIC REGISTRATION FEE

(a) Qualifications: (1) *General:* An applicant for admission to practice before the Court must establish to the satisfaction of the Court that the applicant is of good moral and professional character and possesses the requisite qualifications to provide competent representation before the Court. In addition, the applicant must satisfy the other requirements of this Rule. If the applicant fails to satisfy the requirements of this Rule, then the Court may deny such applicant admission to practice before the Court.

(2) *Attorney Applicants:* An applicant who is an attorney at law must, as a condition of being admitted to practice, file with the Admissions Clerk at the address listed in paragraph (b) of this Rule a completed application accompanied by a fee to be established by the Court, see Appendix II, and a current certificate from the Clerk of the appropriate court, showing that the applicant has been admitted to practice before and is a member in good standing of the Bar of the Supreme Court of the United States, or of the highest or appropriate court of any State or of the District of Columbia, or any commonwealth, territory, or possession of the United States. A current court certificate is one executed within 90 calendar days preceding the date of the filing of the application.

(3) *Nonattorney Applicants:* An applicant who is not an attorney at law must, as a condition of being admitted to practice, file with the Admissions Clerk at the address listed in paragraph (b) of this Rule, a completed application accompanied by a fee to be established by the Court. See Appendix II. In addition, such an applicant must, as a condition of being admitted to practice, satisfy the Court, by means of a written examination given by the Court, that the applicant possesses the requisite qualifications to provide competent representation before the Court. Written examinations for applicants who are not attorneys at law will be held no less often than every 2 years. By public announcement at least 6 months prior to the date of each examination, the Court will announce the date and the time of such examination. The Court will notify each applicant, whose application for admission is in order, of the time and the place at which the applicant is to be present for such examination, and the applicant must present that notice to the examiner as authority for taking such examination.

(b) Applications for Admission: An application for admission to practice before the Court must be on the form provided by the Court. Application forms and other necessary information will be furnished upon request addressed to the Admissions Clerk, United States Tax Court, 400 Second St., N.W., Washington, D.C. 20217. As to forms of payment for application fees, see Rule 11.

(c) Sponsorship: An applicant for admission by examination must be sponsored by at least two persons theretofore admitted to practice before this Court, and each sponsor must send a letter of recommendation directly to the Admissions Clerk at the address listed in paragraph (b) of this Rule, where it will be treated as a confidential communication. The sponsor shall send this letter promptly after the applicant has been notified that he or she has passed the writ- ten examination required by paragraph (a)(3) of this Rule. The sponsor shall state fully and frankly the extent of the sponsor's acquaintance with the applicant, the sponsor's opinion of the moral character and repute of the applicant, and the sponsor's opinion of the qualifications of the applicant to practice before this Court. The Court may in its discretion accept such an applicant with less than two such sponsors.

(d) Admission: Upon the Court's approval of an application for admission in which an applicant has subscribed to the oath or affirmation and upon an applicant's satisfaction of the other applicable requirements of this Rule, such applicant will be admitted to practice before the Court and be entitled to a certificate of admission.

[1]**(e) Change of Address:** Each person admitted to practice before the Court shall promptly notify the Admissions Clerk at the address listed in paragraph (b) of this Rule of any change in office address for mailing purposes. See Form 10 in Appendix I regarding a form for and methods ofproviding the notification required by this paragraph (e). See also Rule 21(b)(4) regarding the filing of a separate notice of change of address for each docket number in which such per- son has entered an appearance.

(f) Corporations and Firms Not Eligible: Corporations and firms will not be admitted to practice or recognized before the Court.

(g) Periodic Registration Fee: (1) Each person admitted to practice before the Court shall pay a periodic registration fee. The frequency and the amount of such fee shall be determined by the Court, except that such amount shall not exceed $30 per calendar year. The Clerk shall maintain an Ineligible List containing the names of all persons admitted to practice before the Court who have failed to comply with the provisions of this paragraph (g)(1). No such person shall be permitted to commence a case in the Court or enter an appearance in a pending case while on the Ineligible List. The name of any person appearing on the Ineligible List shall not be removed from the List until the currently due registration fee has been paid and arrearages have been made current. Each person admitted to practice before the Court, whether or not engaged in private practice, must pay the periodic registration fee. As to forms of payment, see Rule 11.

[1](2) The fees described in paragraph (g)(1) of this Rule shall be used by the Court to compensate independent counsel appointed by the Court to assist it with respect to disciplinary matters. See Rule 202(h).

RULE 201. CONDUCT OF PRACTICE BEFORE THE COURT

(a) General: Practitioners before the Court shall carry on their practice in accordance with the letter and spirit of the Model Rules of Professional Conduct of the American Bar Association.

(b) Statement of Employment: The Court may re- quire any practitioner before it to furnish a statement, under oath, of the terms and circumstances of his or her employ- ment in any case.

RULE 202. DISCIPLINARY MATTERS[1]

(a) General: A member of the Bar of this Court may be disciplined by this Court as a result of:

(1) Conviction in any court of the United States, or of the District of Columbia, or of any State, territory, com- monwealth, or possession of the United States of any felony or of any lesser crime involving false swearing, mis- representation, fraud, criminal violation of any provision of the Internal Revenue Code, bribery, extortion, misappro- priation, theft, or moral turpitude;

(2) Imposition of discipline by any other court of whose bar an attorney is a member, or an attorney's disbarment or suspension by consent or resignation from the bar of such court while an investigation into allegations of mis- conduct is pending;

(3) Conduct with respect to the Court which violates the letter and spirit of the Model Rules of Professional Conduct of the American Bar Association, the Rules of the Court, or orders or other instructions of the Court; or

(4) Any other conduct unbecoming a member of the Bar of the Court.

(b) Reporting Convictions and Discipline: A member of the Bar of this Court who has been convicted of any felony or of any lesser crime described in paragraph (a)(1), who has been disciplined as described in paragraph (a)(2), or who has been disbarred or suspended from practice before an agency of the United States Government exercising professional disciplinary jurisdiction, shall inform the Chair of the Court's Committee on Admissions, Ethics, and Discipline of such action in writing no later than 30 days after entry of   the judgment of conviction or order of discipline.

(c) Disciplinary Actions: Discipline may consist of disbarment, suspension from practice before the Court, reprimand, admonition, or any other sanction that the Court may deem appropriate. The Court may, in the exercise of its discretion, immediately suspend a practitioner from practice before the Court until further order of the Court. Except as provided in paragraph (d), no person shall be suspended for more than 60 days or disbarred until such person has been afforded an opportunity to be heard. A Judge of the Court may immediately suspend any person for not more than 60 days for contempt or misconduct during the course of any trial or hearing.

(d)

(e) Interim Suspension Pending Final Disposition of Disciplinary Proceedings: If a member of the Bar of this Court is convicted in any court of the United States, or of the District of Columbia, or of any State, territory, commonwealth, or possession of the United States of any felony or of any lesser crime described in paragraph (a)(1), then, notwithstanding the pendency of an appeal of the conviction, if any, the Court may, in the exercise of its discretion, immediately suspend such practitioner from practice before the Court pending final disposition of the disciplinary proceedings described in paragraph (e).

(f) Disciplinary Proceedings: Upon the occurrence or allegation of any event described in paragraph (a)(1) through (a)(4), except for any suspension imposed for 60 days or less pursuant to paragraph (c), the Court shall issue to the practitioner an order to show cause why the practitioner should not be disciplined or shall otherwise take appropriate action. The order to show cause shall direct that a written response be filed within such period as the Court may direct and shall set a prompt hearing on the matter before one or more Judges of the Court. If the disciplinary proceeding is predicated upon the complaint of a Judge of the Court, the hearing shall be conducted before a panel of three other Judges of the Court.

(g) Reinstatement: (1) A practitioner suspended for 60 days or less pursuant to paragraph (c) shall be automatically reinstated at the end of the period of suspension.

(2) A practitioner suspended for more than 60 days or disbarred pursuant to this Rule may not resume practice before the Court until reinstated by order of the Court.

(A) A disbarred practitioner or a practitioner suspended for more than 60 days who wishes to be reinstated to practice before the Court must file a petition for reinstatement. Upon receipt of the petition for reinstatement, the Court may set the matter for prompt hearing before one or more Judges of the Court. If the disbarment or suspension for more than 60 days was predicated upon the complaint of a Judge of the Court, any such hearing shall be conducted before a panel of three other Judges of the Court.

(B) In order to be reinstated before the Court, the practitioner must demonstrate by clear and convincing evidence in the petition for reinstatement and at any hearing that such practitioner's reinstatement will not be detrimental to the integrity and standing of the Court's Bar or to the administration of justice, or subversive of the public interest.

(C) No petition for reinstatement under this Rule shall be filed within 1 year following an adverse decision upon a petition for reinstatement filed by or on behalf of the same person.

(h) Right to Counsel: In all proceedings conducted under the provisions of this Rule, the practitioner shall have the right to be represented by counsel.

(i) Appointment of Court Counsel: The Court, in its discretion, may appoint counsel to the Court to assist it with respect to any disciplinary matters.

(j) Jurisdiction: Nothing contained in this Rule shall be construed to deny to the Court such powers as are necessary for the Court to maintain control over proceedings conducted before it, such as proceedings for contempt under Code section 7456 or for costs under Code section 6673(a)(2).

TITLE XXI DECLARATORY JUDGMENTS

RULE 210. GENERAL

(a) Applicability: The Rules of this Title XXI set forth the special provisions which apply to declaratory judgment actions relating to the qualification of certain retirement plans, the value of certain gifts, the status of certain govern- mental obligations, the eligibility of an estate with respect to installment payments under Code section 6166, and the initial or continuing qualification of certain exempt organizations or the initial or continuing classification of certain private foundations. For the Rules that apply to declaratory judgment actions relating to treatment of items other than partnership items with respect to an oversheltered return, see the Rules contained in Title XXX. Except as otherwise provided in this Title, the other Rules of Practice and Procedure of the Court, to the extent pertinent, are applicable to such actions for declaratory judgment.

(b) Definitions: As used in the Rules in this Title—

(1) ''Retirement plan'' has the meaning provided by Code section 7476(c).

(2) A ''gift'' is any transfer of property that was shown on the return of tax imposed by Code chapter 12 or dis- closed on

such return or in any statement attached to such return.

(3) "Governmental obligation" means an obligation the status of which under Code section 103(a) is in issue.

(4) An "estate" is any estate whose initial or continuing eligibility with respect to the deferral and installment payment election under Code section 6166 is in issue.

(5) An "exempt organization" is an organization described in Code section 501(c)(3) which is exempt from tax under Code section 501(a) or is an organization described in Code section 170(c)(2).

(6) A "private foundation" is an organization described in Code section 509(a).

(7) A "private operating foundation" is an organization described in Code section 4942(j)(3).

(8) An "organization" is any organization whose qualification as an exempt organization, or whose classificationas a private foundation or a private operating foundation, is in issue.

(9) A "determination" means—

(A) A determination with respect to the initial or continuing qualification of a retirement plan;

(B) a determination of the value of any gift;

(C) a determination as to whether prospective governmental obligations are described in Code section 103(a);

(D) a determination as to whether, with respect to an estate, an election may be made under Code section 6166 or whether the extension of time for payment of estate tax provided in Code section 6166 has ceased to apply; or

(E) a determination with respect to the initial or continuing qualification of an organization as an exempt organization, or with respect to the initial or continuing classification of an organization as a private foundation or a private operating foundation.

(10) A "revocation" is a determination that a retirement plan is no longer qualified, or that an organization, previously qualified or classified as an exempt organization or as a private foundation or private operating foundation, is no longer qualified or classified as such an organization.

(11) An "action for declaratory judgment" is either a retirement plan action, a gift valuation action, a govern- mental obligation action, an estate tax installment payment action, or an exempt organization action, as follows:

(A) A "retirement plan action" means an action for declaratory judgment provided for in Code section 7476 relating to the initial or continuing qualification of a retirement plan.

(B) A "gift valuation action" means an action for declaratory judgment provided for in Code section 7477 relating to the valuation of a gift.

(C) A "governmental obligation action" means an action for declaratory judgment provided for in Code section 7478 relating to the status of certain prospective governmental obligations.

(D) An "estate tax installment payment action" means an action for declaratory judgment provided for in Code section 7479 relating to the eligibility of an estatewith respect to installment payments under Code section 6166.

(E) An "exempt organization action" means a declaratory judgment action provided for in Code section 7428 relating to the initial or continuing qualification of an organization as an exempt organization, or relating to the initial or continuing classification of an organization as a private foundation or a private operating foundation.

(12) "Administrative record" includes, where applicable, the request for determination, all documents submitted to the Internal Revenue Service by the applicant in respect of the request for determination, all protests and related pa- pers submitted to the Internal Revenue Service, all written correspondence between the Internal Revenue Service and the applicant in respect of the request for determination of such protests, all pertinent returns filed with the Internal Revenue Service, and the notice of determination by the Commissioner.

(13) "Party" includes a petitioner and the respondent Commissioner of Internal Revenue. In a retirement plan action, an intervenor is also a party. In a gift valuation action, only the donor may be a petitioner. In a governmental obligation action, only the prospective issuer may be a petitioner. In an estate tax installment payment action, a per- son joined pursuant to Code section 7479(b)(1)(B) is also a party. In an exempt organization action, only the organization may be a petitioner.

(14) "Declaratory judgment" is the decision of the Court in a retirement plan action, a gift valuation action, a governmental obligation action, an estate tax installment payment action, or an exempt organization action.

(c) **Jurisdictional Requirements:** The Court does not have jurisdiction of an action for declaratory judgment under this Title unless the following conditions are satisfied:

(1) The Commissioner has issued a notice of determination, or has been requested to make a determination and failed to do so for a period of at least 270 days (180 days in the case of either a request for determination as to the status of prospective governmental obligations or a request for determination as to the initial or continuing eligibility of an estate with respect to installment payments under Code section 6166) after the request for such determination was made. In the case of a retirement plan action, the Court has

104

jurisdiction over an action brought because of the Commissioner's failure to make a determination with respect to the continuing qualification of the plan only if the controversy arises as a result of an amendment or termination of such plan. See Code sec. 7476(a)(2)(B). In the case of a gift valuation action, the Court has jurisdiction if the Commissioner has issued a notice of determination. See Code sec. 7477(a).

(2) There is an actual controversy. In that connection—

(A) In the case of a retirement plan action, the retirement plan or amendment thereto in issue has been put into effect before commencement of the action.

(B) In the case of a governmental obligation action, the prospective issuer has, prior to the commencement of the action, adopted an appropriate resolution in accordance with State or local law authorizing the issuance of such obligations.

(C) In the case of an exempt organization action, the organization must be in existence before commencement of the action.

(3) A petition for declaratory judgment is filed with the Court within the period specified in Code section 7476(b)(5) with respect to a retirement plan action, or the period specified in Code section 7477(b)(3) with respect to a gift valuation action, or the period specified in Code section 7478(b)(3) with respect to a governmental obligation action, or the period specified in Code section 7479(b)(3) with respect to an estate tax installment payment action, or the period specified in Code section 7428(b)(3) with respect to an exempt organization action. See Code sec. 7502.

(4) The petitioner has exhausted all administrative remedies which were available to the petitioner within the Internal Revenue Service.

(d) Form and Style of Papers: All papers filed in an action for declaratory judgment, with the exception of documents included in the administrative record, shall be pre- pared in the form and style set forth in Rule 23; except that whenever any party joins or intervenes in the action in those instances in which joinder or intervention is permitted, then thereafter, in addition to the number of copies required to be filed under such Rule, an additional copy shall be filed for each party who joins or intervenes in the action.

RULE 211. COMMENCEMENT OF ACTION FOR DECLARATORY JUDGMENT

(a) Commencement of Action: An action for declaratory judgment shall be commenced by filing a petition with the

Court. See Rule 22, relating to the place and manner of filing the petition, and Rule 32, relating to form of pleadings.

(b) Content of Petition: Every petition shall be entitled "Petition for Declaratory Judgment (Retirement Plan)", "Petition for Declaratory Judgment (Gift Valuation)", "Petition for Declaratory Judgment (Governmental Obligation)", "Petition for Declaratory Judgment (Estate Tax Installment Payment)", or "Petition for Declaratory Judgment (Exempt Organization)", as the case may be. Each such petition shall contain the allegations described in paragraph (c), (d), (e), (f), or (g) of this Rule. A claim for reasonable litigation or administrative costs shall not be included in the petition in a declaratory judgment action. For the requirements as to claims for reasonable litigation or administrative costs, see Rule 231.

(c) Petition in Retirement Plan Action: The petition in a retirement plan action shall contain:

(1) *All Petitions:* All petitions in retirement plan actions shall contain the following:

(A) The petitioner's name and address, and the name and principal place of business, or principal office or agency of the employer at the time the petition is filed; and

(B) the office of the Internal Revenue Service with which the request for determination, if any, was filed and the date of such filing.

(2) *Employer Petitions:* In addition to including the information described in paragraph (c)(1) of this Rule, a petition filed by an employer shall also contain:

(A) A separate numbered paragraph stating that the employer has complied with the requirements of the regulations issued under Code section 7476(b)(2) with respect to notice to other interested parties;

(B) a separate numbered paragraph stating that the employer has exhausted the employer's administrative remedies within the Internal Revenue Service;

(C) a separate numbered paragraph stating that the retirement plan has been put into effect in accordance with Code section 7476(b)(4);

(D) where the Commissioner has issued a notice of determination that the retirement plan does not qualify—

(i) the date of the notice of the Commissioner's determination,

(ii) a copy of such notice of determination,

(iii) in a separate numbered paragraph, a clear and concise assignment of each error, set forth in a separate lettered subparagraph, which the employer alleges to have been committed by the Commissioner in the determination, and

(iv) a statement of facts upon which the petitioner

106

relies to support each such claim;

(E)   where the Commissioner has not issued a notice of determination with respect to the qualification of the retirement plan, separate numbered paragraphs stating that—

(i)   the requested determination is of the type described in Code section 7476(a)(1) or (2),

(ii)   no determination has been made by the Commissioner in response thereto, and

(iii)   the retirement plan does qualify;

(F)   an appropriate prayer for relief; and

(G)   the signature, mailing address, and telephone number of each petitioner or each petitioner's counsel, as well as counsel's Tax Court bar number.

(3)   *Petitions Filed by Plan Administrators:* In addition to including the information specified in paragraph (c)(1) of this Rule, a petition filed by a plan administrator shall contain:

(A)   The name, address, and principal place of business, or principal office or agency, of the employer who is required to contribute under the plan; and

(B)   in separate numbered paragraphs, the statements or information required in the case of employer petitions in paragraph (c)(2) of this Rule.

(4)   *Employee Petitions:* In addition to including the information specified in paragraph (c)(1) of this Rule, a petition filed by an employee shall also contain:

(A)   A separate numbered paragraph setting forth a statement that the employee has qualified as an interested party in accordance with the regulations issued under Code section 7476(b)(1);

(B)   in separate numbered paragraphs, the statements described in subparagraph (2)(B) and (C) of paragraph (c) of this Rule;

(C)   where the Commissioner has issued a notice of determination that the retirement plan does not qualify,   a copy of such notice of determination, and in separate numbered paragraphs, the statements described in subparagraph (2)(D)(i), (iii), and (iv) of paragraph (c) of this Rule;

(D)   where the Commissioner has issued a notice of determination that a retirement plan does qualify, a copy of such notice of determination, and in separate numbered paragraphs, the date of such notice of determination, and a clear and concise statement of each ground, set forth in a separate lettered subparagraph, upon which the employee relies to assert that such plan does   not qualify and the facts to support each ground;

(E)   where the Commissioner has not issued a notice of determination with respect to the qualification of the retirement plan, a statement, in a separate numbered paragraph, as to whether the retirement plan qualifies—

(i) if the employee alleges that the retirement plan does qualify, such paragraph shall also include the statements described in paragraph (c)(2)(E) of this Rule, or

(ii) if the employee alleges that the retirement plan does not qualify, in addition to the statements described in paragraph (c)(2)(E) of this Rule, such paragraph shall also include a clear and concise statement of each ground, in a separate lettered subparagraph, upon which the employee relies to support the allegation that such plan does not qualify and the facts relied upon to support each ground; and

(F) in separate numbered paragraphs, the statements described in paragraph (c)(2)(F) and (G) of this Rule.(5) *Petitions Filed by the Pension Benefit Guaranty Corporation:* In addition to including the information specified in paragraph (c)(1) of this Rule, a petition filed by the Pension Benefit Guaranty Corporation shall also contain in separate numbered paragraphs the statements described in paragraph (c)(4)(B), (C), (D), (E), and (F) of this Rule.

(d) **Petition in Gift Valuation Action:** The petition in a gift valuation action shall contain:

(1) The petitioner's name, State of legal residence, and mailing address;

(2) a statement that the petitioner is the donor of a gift described in Code section 7477(a);

(3) a statement that the petitioner has exhausted all administrative remedies within the Internal Revenue Service;

(4) with respect to the Commissioner's notice of determination—

(A) the date of the notice of determination;

(B) a copy of the notice of determination;

(C) in a separate numbered paragraph, a clear and concise statement of each error, in separate lettered subparagraphs, which the petitioner alleges to have been committed by the Commissioner in the determination; and

(D) a statement of facts upon which the petitioner relies to support each such claim;

(5) an appropriate prayer for relief; and

(6) the signature, mailing address, and telephone number of the petitioner or petitioner's counsel, as well as counsel's Tax Court bar number.

(e) **Petition in Governmental Obligation Action:** The petition in a governmental obligation action shall contain:

(1) The petitioner's name and address;

(2) the office of the Internal Revenue Service with which the request for determination was filed and the date of such

filing;

(3) a statement that the petitioner is a prospective issuer of governmental obligations described in Code section 103(a) which has adopted an appropriate resolution in accordance with State or local law authorizing the issuance of such obligations;

(4) a statement that the petitioner has exhausted its administrative remedies;

(5) where the Commissioner has issued a determination—

(A) the date of the notice of determination;

(B) a copy of such notice of determination;

(C) in a separate numbered paragraph, a clear and concise statement of each error, in separate lettered subparagraphs, which the petitioner alleges to have been committed by the Commissioner in the determination; and

(D) a statement of facts upon which the petitioner relies to support each such claim;

(6) where the Commissioner has not issued a notice of determination, separate numbered paragraphs stating that—

(A) no such determination has been made by the Commissioner; and

(B) the prospective governmental obligations are described in Code section 103(a);

(7) an appropriate prayer for relief; and

(8) the signature, mailing address, and telephone number of the petitioner or its counsel, as well as counsel's Tax Court bar number.

(f) **Petition in Estate Tax Installment Payment Action:** The petition in an estate tax installment payment action shall contain:

(1) All Petitions:

(A) The petitioner's name and address;

(B) the decedent's name and State of legal residence at the date of death, and the jurisdiction in which the estate was admitted to probate;

(C) the office of the Internal Revenue Service with which the request for determination, if any, was filed and the date of such filing; and

(D) a statement that the petitioner has exhausted all available administrative remedies within the Internal Revenue Service;

(E) where the Commissioner has issued a determination either that the estate may not make the election under Code section 6166 or that the extension of time for

payment of tax provided in Code section 6166 has ceased to apply with respect to the estate—

(i)   the date of the notice of the Commissioner's determination,

(ii)   a copy of such notice of determination,

(iii)   in a separate numbered paragraph, a clear and concise assignment of each error, set forth in a separate lettered subparagraph, which the petitioner alleges to have been committed by the Commissioner in the determination, and

(iv)   a statement of facts upon which the petitioner relies to support each such claim;

(F)   where the Commissioner has not issued a notice of determination as to the initial or continuing eligibility of the estate with respect to installment payments under Code section 6166, separate numbered paragraphs stating that—

(i)   the requested determination is of the type described in Code section 7479(a)(1) or (2),

(ii)   no determination has been made by the Commissioner in response thereto, and

(iii)   the estate is eligible;

(G)   an appropriate prayer for relief; and

(H)   the signature, mailing address, and telephone number of petitioner or petitioner's counsel, as well as counsel's Tax Court bar number.

(2)   *Petitions Filed by Executors:* In addition to including the information specified in paragraph (f)(1) of this Rule, a petition filed by an estate's executor shall contain   a separate numbered paragraph stating that the petition   has been filed on behalf of an executor.

(3)   *Petitions Filed by Persons Who Have Assumed an Obligation To Make Payments Under Code Section 6166:* In addition to including the information specified in para- graph (f)(1) of this Rule, a petition filed by a person, or persons, who has, or have, assumed an obligation to make payments under Code section 6166 with respect to an es- tate shall also contain:

(A)   A separate numbered paragraph stating that the person, or persons, has, or have, assumed an obligation to make payments under Code section 6166 with respect to the estate; and

(B)   in a separate numbered paragraph, the name and address of each other person who has assumed such obligation and is not a party to the action.

(g)   **Petition in Exempt Organization Action:** The petition in an exempt organization action shall contain:

(1)   The petitioner's name and principal place of business or principal office or agency;

(2)   the date upon which the request for determination, if any, was mailed to the Internal Revenue Service, and the

office to which it was mailed;

(3) a statement that the petitioner is an exempt organization or a private foundation or a private operating foundation, as the case may be, the qualification or classification of which is at issue;

(4) a statement that the petitioner has exhausted its administrative remedies within the Internal Revenue Service;

(5) where the Commissioner has issued a determination—

(A) the date of the notice of determination;

(B) a copy of such notice of determination;

(C) in a separate numbered paragraph, a clear and concise statement of each reason, in separate lettered subparagraphs, why the determination is erroneous; and

(D) a statement of facts upon which petitioner relies to support each of such reasons;

(6) where the Commissioner has not issued a notice of determination, separate numbered paragraphs stating that—

(A) no such determination has been made by the Commissioner; and

(B) the organization is qualified under Code section 501(c)(3) or 170(c)(2), or should be classified with respect to Code section 509(a) or 4942(j)(3) in the manner set forth by the petitioner in its request for determination;

(7) an appropriate prayer for relief; and

(8) the signature, mailing address, and telephone number of the petitioner or its counsel, as well as counsel's Tax Court bar number.

(h) **Service:** For the provisions relating to service of the petition and other papers, see Rule 21.

RULE 212. REQUEST FOR PLACE FOR SUBMISSION TO THE COURT

At the time of filing a petition for a declaratory judgment, a request for place for submission to the Court shall be filed in accordance with Rule 140. In addition to including in the request the information specified in Rule 140, the petitioner shall also include the date on which the petitioner expects the action will be ready for submission to the Court and the petitioner's estimate of the time required therefor. In cases involving a revocation or involving the status of a governmental obligation, the Commissioner shall, at the time the answer is filed, also set forth in a separate statement the date on which the Commissioner expects the action will be ready for submission to the Court and an estimate of the time required therefor. After the action becomes at issue (see Rule 214), it will ordinarily, without any further request by the Court for information as to readiness for submission, be placed on a calendar for submission to the Court. See Rule 217(b).

RULE 213. OTHER PLEADINGS

(a) Answer: (1) *Time To Answer or Move:* The Commissioner shall have 60 days from the date of service of the petition within which to file an answer, or 45 days from that date within which to move with respect to the petition. With respect to an amended petition or amendments to the petition, the Commissioner shall have like time periods from the date of service of those papers within which to answer or move in response thereto, except as the Court may otherwise direct.

(2) *Form and Content:* The answer shall be drawn so that it will advise the petitioner and the Court fully of the nature of the defense. It shall contain a specific admission or denial of each material allegation of the petition. If the Commissioner shall be without knowledge or information sufficient to form a belief as to the truth of an allegation as to jurisdictional facts or as to inferences or conclusions that may be drawn from materials in the administrative record or as to facts involved in a revocation, then the Commissioner may so state, and such statement shall have the effect of a denial. Facts other than jurisdictional facts, and other than facts involved in a revocation or in a governmental obligation action, may be admitted only for purposes of the pending action for declaratory judgment. If the Commissioner intends to clarify or to deny only a part of an allegation, then the Commissioner shall specify so much of it as is true and shall qualify or deny only the remain- der. In addition, the answer shall contain a clear and concise statement of every ground, together with the facts in support thereof, on which the Commissioner relies and has the burden of proof. Paragraphs of the answer shall be designated to correspond to those of the petition to which they relate.

(3) *Index to Administrative Record:* In addition, the answer shall contain an affirmative allegation that attached thereto is a complete index of the contents of the administrative record to be filed with the Court. See Rule 217(b). There shall be attached to the answer such complete index.

(4) *Effect of Answer:* Every material allegation set out in the petition and not expressly admitted or denied in the answer shall be deemed to be admitted.

(b) Reply: Each petitioner shall file a reply in every action for declaratory judgment.

(1) *Time To Reply or Move:* The petitioner shall have 60 days from the date of service of the answer within which to file a reply, or 30 days from that date within which to move with respect to the answer. With respect to an amended answer or amendments to the answer, the pe-

titioner shall have like periods from the date of service of those papers within which to reply or move in response thereto, except as the Court may otherwise direct.

(2) *Form and Content:* In response to each material allegation in the answer and the facts in support thereof on which the Commissioner has the burden of proof, the reply shall contain a specific admission or denial; however, if the petitioner shall be without knowledge or information sufficient to form a belief as to the truth of an allegation, then the petitioner shall so state, and such statement shall have the effect of a denial. If the petitioner denies the affirmative allegation in the answer that a complete index of the contents of the administrative record is attached to the answer, then the petitioner shall specify the reasons forsuch denial. In addition, the reply shall contain a clear and concise statement of every ground, together with the facts in support thereof, on which the petitioner relies affirmatively or in avoidance of any matter in the answer on which the Commissioner has the burden of proof. In other respects, the requirements of pleading applicable to the answer provided in paragraph (a)(2) of this Rule shall apply to the reply. The paragraphs of the reply shall be designated to correspond to those of the answer to which they relate.

(3) *Effect of Reply or Failure Thereof:* Where a reply is filed, every affirmative allegation set out in the answer and not expressly admitted or denied in the reply shall be deemed to be admitted. Where a reply is not filed, the affirmative allegations in the answer will be deemed admit- ted.

(4) *New Material:* Any new material contained in the reply shall be deemed to be denied.

RULE 214. JOINDER OF ISSUE IN ACTION FOR DECLARATORY JUDGMENT

An action for declaratory judgment shall be deemed at issue upon the filing of the reply or at the expiration of the time for doing so.

RULE 215. JOINDER OF PARTIES

(a) Joinder in Retirement Plan Action: The joinder of parties in retirement plan actions shall be subject to the following requirements:

(1) *Permissive Joinder:* Any person who, under Code section 7476(b)(1), is entitled to commence an action for declaratory judgment with respect to the qualification of a retirement plan may join in filing a petition with any other such person in such an action with respect to the same plan. If the Commissioner has issued a notice of determination with respect to the qualification of the plan, then any person

joining in the petition must do so within the period specified in Code section 7476(b)(5). If more than one petition is filed with respect to the qualification of the same retirement plan, then see Rule 141 (relating to the possibility of consolidating the actions with respect to the plan).

[1](2) *Joinder of Additional Parties:* Any party to an action for declaratory judgment with respect to the qualification of a retirement plan may move to have joined in the action any employer who established or maintains the plan, plan administrator, or any person in whose absence complete relief cannot be accorded among those already parties. Unless otherwise permitted by the Court, any such motion must be filed not later than 30 days after joinder of issue. See Rule 214. In addition to serving the parties to the action, the movant shall cause personal service to be made on each person sought to be joined by a United States marshal or by a deputy marshal, or by any other person who is not a party and is not less than 18 years of age, who shall make a return of service. See Form 9, Appendix I. Such return of service shall be filed with the motion, but failure to do so or otherwise to make proof of service does not affect the validity of the service. Unless otherwise permitted by the Court, any objection to such motion shall be filed within 30 days after the service of the motion. The motion will be granted whenever the Court finds that in the interests of justice such person should be joined. If the motion is granted, such person will thereupon become a party to the action, and the Court will enter such orders as it deems appropriate as to further pleading and other matters. See Rule 50(b) with respect to actions on motions.

(3) *Nonjoinder of Necessary Parties:* If the Court determines that any person described in subparagraph (2) of this paragraph is a necessary party to an action for declaratory judgment and that such person has not been joined, then the Court may, on its own motion or on the motion of any party or any such person, dismiss the action on the ground that the absent person is necessary and that justice cannot be accomplished in the absent person's absence, or direct that any such person be made a party to the action. An order dismissing a case for nonjoinder of a necessary party may be conditional or absolute.

Joinder in Estate Tax Installment Payment Action: The joinder of parties in estate tax installment payment actions shall be subject to the following requirements:

(1) *Permissive Joinder:* Any person who, under Code section 7479(b)(1), is entitled to commence an action for declaratory judgment relating to the eligibility of an estate with respect to installment payments under Code section 6166 may join in filing a petition with any other such person in such an action with respect to such estate. If the

114

Commissioner has issued a notice of determination with respect to the eligibility of the estate, then any person joining in the petition must do so within the period specified in Code section 7479(b)(3). If more than one petition is filed with respect to the eligibility of the same estate, then see Rule 141 (relating to the possibility of consolidating the actions with respect to the estate).

[1](2) *Joinder of Additional Parties:* Any party to an action for declaratory judgment relating to the eligibility of   an estate with respect to installment payments under Code section 6166 may move to have joined in the action any executor or any person who has assumed an obligation to make payments under Code section 6166 with respect to such estate. Unless otherwise permitted by the Court, any such motion must be filed not later than 30 days after join- der of issue. See Rule 214. In addition to serving the par- ties to the action, the movant shall cause personal service   to be made on each person sought to be joined by a United States marshal or by a deputy marshal, or by any other person who is not a party and is not less than 18 years of age, who shall make a return of service. See Form 9, Appendix I. Such return of service shall be filed with the motion, but failure to do so or otherwise to make proof of service does not affect the validity of the service. Unless otherwise permitted by the Court, any objection to such motion shall be filed within 30 days after the service of the motion. The motion will be granted whenever the Court finds that in the interests of justice such person should be joined. If the motion is granted, such person will thereupon become a party to the action, and the Court will enter such orders as it deems appropriate as to further pleading and other matters. See Rule 50(b) with respect to actions on motions.

(3) *Nonjoinder of Necessary Parties:* If the Court determines that any person described in subparagraph (2) of this paragraph is a necessary party to an action for declaratory judgment, or, in the case of an action brought by a person described in Code section 7479(b)(1)(B), is another such person described in Code section 7479(b)(1)(B), and that such person has not been joined, then the Court may, on its own motion or on the motion of any party or any such person, dismiss the action on the ground that the absent person is necessary and that justice cannot be accomplished in the absence of such person, or direct that any such person be made a party to the action. An order dismissing a case for nonjoinder of a necessary party may be conditional or absolute.

(c) Joinder of Parties in Gift Valuation, Governmental Obligation, and Exempt Organization Actions: Joinder of parties is not permitted in a gift valuation action,   in a governmental obligation action, or in an exempt organization action. See Code secs. 7477(b)(1), 7478(b)(1), 7428(b)(1). With respect to consolidation of actions, see Rule 141.

RULE 216. INTERVENTION IN RETIREMENT PLAN ACTIONS

(a) **Who May Intervene:** The Pension Benefit Guaranty Corporation and, if entitled to intervene pursuant to the provisions of section 3001(c) of the Employee Retirement Income Security Act of 1974, the Secretary of Labor, or either of them, shall be permitted to intervene in a retirement plan action in accordance with the provisions of Code section 7476.

(b) **Procedure:** If either of the persons mentioned in paragraph (a) of this Rule desires to intervene, then such person shall file a pleading, either a petition in intervention or an answer in intervention, not later than 30 days after joinder of issue (see Rule 214) unless the Court directs otherwise. All new matters of claim or defense in a pleading in intervention shall be deemed denied.

RULE 217. DISPOSITION OF ACTIONS FOR DECLARATORY JUDGMENT

(a) **General:** Disposition of an action for declaratory judgment which involves the initial qualification of a retirement plan or the initial qualification or classification of an exempt organization, a private foundation, or a private operating foundation will ordinarily be made on the basis of the administrative record, as defined in Rule 210(b)(12). Only with the permission of the Court, upon good cause shown, will any party be permitted to introduce before the Court any evidence other than that presented before the Internal Revenue Service and contained in the administrative record as so defined. Disposition of an action for declaratory judgment involving a revocation, a gift valuation, or the eligibility of an estate with respect to installment payments under Code section 6166 may be made on the basis of the administrative record alone only where the parties agree that such record contains all the relevant facts and that such facts are not in dispute. Disposition of a governmental obligation action will be made on the basis of the administrative record, augmented by additional evidence to the extent that the Court may direct.

(b) **Procedure:** (1) *Disposition on the Administrative Record:* Within 30 days after service of the answer, the parties shall file with the Court the entire administrative record (or so much thereof as either party may deem necessary for a complete disposition of the action for declaratory judgment), stipulated as to its genuineness. If, however, the parties are unable to file such a stipulated administrative record, then, not sooner than 30 days nor later than 45 days after service of the answer, the Commissioner shall file with the Court the entire administrative record, as defined in Rule 210(b)(12), appropriately certified as to its genuineness by the Commissioner or by an official authorized to act for the Commissioner in such situation. See Rule 212, as to the time and place for submission of the action to the Court. The Court will thereafter issue an opinion and declaratory judgment in the action. In an action involving the initial qualification of a retirement plan or the initial qualification or classification of an exempt organization, a private foundation, or a private operating foundation, the Court's decision will be based upon the assumption that the facts as represented in the administrative record as so stipulated or so certified are true and upon any additional facts as found by the Court if the Court deems that a trial is necessary. In an action involving a gift valuation, the eligibility of an estate with respect to installment payments under Code section 6166, a revocation, or the status of a governmental obliga- tion, the Court may, upon the basis of the evidence pre- sented, make findings of fact which differ from the adminis- trative record.

(2) *Other Dispositions Without Trial:* In addition, an action for declaratory judgment may be decided on a mo- tion for a judgment on the pleadings under Rule 120 or on a motion for summary judgment under Rule 121 or such an action may be submitted at any time by notice of the par- ties filed with the Court in accordance with Rule 122.

(3) *Disposition Where Trial Is Required:* Whenever a trial is required in an action for declaratory judgment, such trial shall be conducted in accordance with the Rules contained in Title XIV, except as otherwise provided in this Title.

RULE 218. PROCEDURE IN ACTIONS HEARD BY A SPECIAL TRIAL JUDGE OF THE COURT

(a) Where the Special Trial Judge Is To Make the Decision: When an action for declaratory judgment is as- signed to a Special Trial Judge who is authorized in the order of assignment to make the decision, the opinion and proposed decision of the Special Trial Judge shall be sub- mitted to and approved by the Chief Judge or by another Judge designated by the Chief Judge for that purpose, prior to service of the opinion and decision upon the parties.

(b) Where the Special Trial Judge Is Not To Make the Decision: Where an action for declaratory judgment is assigned to a Special Trial Judge who is not authorized in the order of assignment to make the decision, the procedure provided in Rule 183 shall be followed.

TITLE XXII

DISCLOSURE ACTIONS

RULE 220. GENERAL

(a) Applicability: The Rules of this Title XXII set forth the special provisions which apply to the three types of dis- closure actions relating to written determinations by the Internal Revenue Service and their background file documents, as authorized by Code section 6110. They consist of: (1) Actions to restrain disclosure, (2) actions to obtain additional disclosure, and (3) actions to obtain disclosure of identity in the case of third party contacts. Except as otherwise provided in this Title, the other Rules of Practice and Procedure of the Court, to the extent pertinent, are applicable to such disclosure actions.

(b) Definitions: As used in the Rules in this Title—

(1) A "written determination" means a ruling, determination letter, or technical advice memorandum. See Code sec. 6110(b)(1).

(2) A "prior written determination" is a written determination issued pursuant to a request made before November 1, 1976.

(3) A "background file document" has the meaning provided in Code section 6110(b)(2).

(4) A "notice of intention to disclose" is the notice described in Code section 6110(f)(1).

(5) "Party" includes a petitioner, the respondent Commissioner of Internal Revenue, and any intervenor under Rule 225.

(6) A "disclosure action" is either an "additional disclosure action", an "action to restrain disclosure", or a "third party contact action", as follows:

(A) An "additional disclosure action" is an action to obtain disclosure within Code section 6110(f)(4).

(B) An "action to restrain disclosure" is an action within Code section 6110(f)(3) or (h)(4) to prevent any part or all of a written determination, prior written determination, or background file document from being opened to public inspection.

(C) A "third party contact action" is an action to obtain disclosure of the identity of a person to whom a

written determination pertains in accordance with Code section 6110(d)(3).

(7) "Third party contact" means the person described in Code section 6110(d)(1) who has communicated with the Internal Revenue Service.

(c) Jurisdictional Requirements: The Court does not have jurisdiction of a disclosure action under this Title unless the following conditions are satisfied:

(1) In an additional disclosure action, the petitioner has

exhausted all administrative remedies available within the Internal Revenue Service. See Code sec. 6110(f)(2)(A), (4)(A).

(2) In an action to restrain disclosure—

(A) The Commissioner has issued a notice of intention to disclose or, in the case of a prior written determination, the Commissioner has issued public notice in the Federal Register that the determination is to be opened to public inspection.

(B) In the case of a written determination, the petition is filed with the Court within 60 days after mailing by the Commissioner of a notice of intention to disclose, or, in the case of a prior written determination, the petition is filed with the Court within 75 days after the date of publication of the notice in the Federal Register.

(C) The petitioner has exhausted all administrative remedies available within the Internal Revenue Service. See Code sec. 6110(f)(2)(B), (3)(A)(iii).

(3) In a third party contact action—

(A) The Commissioner was required to make a notation on the written determination in accordance with Code section 6110(d)(1).

(B) A petition is filed within 36 months after the first date on which the written determination is open to public inspection.

(d) Form and Style of Papers: All papers filed in a disclosure action shall be prepared in the form and style set forth in Rule 23, except that whenever any party joins or intervenes in the action, then thereafter, in addition to the number of copies required to be filed under such Rule, an additional copy shall be filed for each party who joins or intervenes in the action. In the case of anonymous parties, see Rule 227.

(e)

RULE 221. COMMENCEMENT OF DISCLOSURE ACTION

(a) Commencement of Action: A disclosure action shall be commenced by filing a petition with the Court. See Rule 22, relating to the place and manner of filing the petition, and Rule 32, relating to the form of pleadings.

(b) Content of Petition: Every petition shall be entitled "Petition for Additional Disclosure" or "Petition To Re- strain Disclosure" or "Petition To Disclose Identity". Subject to the provisions of Rule 227, dealing with anonymity, each petition shall contain the petitioner's name and State of legal residence, an appropriate prayer for relief, and the signature, mailing address, and telephone number of the petitioner or the petitioner's counsel, as well as counsel's Tax Court bar number. In addition, each petition shall contain the allegations described in paragraph (c), (d), or (e) of this Rule.

119

(c) Petition in Additional Disclosure Action: The petition in an additional disclosure action shall contain:

(1) A brief description (including any identifying number or symbol) of the written determination, prior written determination, or background file document, as to which the petitioner seeks additional disclosure. A copy of any such determination or document, as it is then available to the public, shall be appended.

(2) The date of the petitioner's request to the Internal Revenue Service for additional disclosure, with a copy of such request appended.

(3) A statement of the Commissioner's disposition of the request, with a copy of the disposition appended.

(4) A statement that the petitioner has exhausted all administrative remedies available within the Internal Revenue Service.

(5) In separate lettered subparagraphs, a clear and concise statement identifying each portion of the written determination, prior written determination, or background file document as to which the petitioner seeks additional disclosure together with any facts and reasons to support disclosure. See Rule 229 with respect to the burden of proof in an additional disclosure action.

(d) Petition in Action To Restrain Disclosure: The petition in an action to restrain disclosure shall contain:

(1) A statement that the petitioner is: (A) A person to whom the written determination pertains; (B) a successor in interest, executor, or other person authorized by law to act for or on behalf of such person; (C) a person who has a direct interest in maintaining the confidentiality of the written determination or background file document or portion thereof; or (D) in the case of a prior written determination, the person who received such prior written determination.

(2) A statement that the Commissioner has issued a notice of intention to disclose with respect to a written determination or a background file document, stating the date of mailing of the notice of intention to disclose and appending a copy of it to the petition, or, in the case of a prior written determination, a statement that the Commissioner has issued public notice in the Federal Register that the determination is to be opened to public inspection, and stating the date and citation of such publication in the Federal Register.

(3) A brief description (including any identifying number or symbol) of the written determination, prior written determination, or background file document, as to which the petitioner seeks to restrain disclosure.

(4) The date of the petitioner's request to the Internal Revenue Service to refrain from disclosure, with a copy of

such request appended.

(5) A statement of the Commissioner's disposition of the request, with a copy of such disposition appended.

(6) A statement that the petitioner has exhausted all administrative remedies available within the Internal Revenue Service.

(7) In separate lettered subparagraphs, a clear and concise statement identifying each portion of the written determination, prior written determination, or background file document as to which the petitioner seeks to restrain disclosure, together with any facts and reasons to support the petitioner's position. See Rule 229 with respect to the burden of proof in an action to restrain disclosure.

(e) Petition in Third Party Contact Action: The petition in a third party contact action shall contain:

(1) A brief description (including any identifying number or symbol) of the written determination to which the action pertains. There shall be appended a copy of such determination, and the background file document (if any) reflecting the third party contact, as then available to the public.

(2) The date of the first day that the written determination was open to public inspection.

(3) A statement of the disclosure sought by the petitioner.

(4) A clear and concise statement of the impropriety alleged to have occurred or the undue influence alleged to have been exercised with respect to the written determination or on behalf of the person whose identity is sought, and the public interest supporting any other disclosure. See Rule 229 with respect to the burden of proof in a third party contact action.

(f) Service: For the provisions relating to service of the petition and other papers, see Rule 21.

(g) Anonymity: With respect to anonymous pleading, see Rule 227.

RULE 222. REQUEST FOR PLACE OF HEARING

At the time of filing a petition in a disclosure action, a request for a place of hearing shall be filed in accordance with Rule 140. In addition, the petitioner shall include the date on which the petitioner believes the action will be ready for submission to the Court and the petitioner's estimate of the time required therefor. The Commissioner shall, at the time the answer is filed, also set forth in a separate statement the date on which the Commissioner expects the action will be ready for submission to the Court and an estimate of the time required therefor. An intervenor shall likewise furnish such information to the Court in a separate statement filed with the intervenor's first pleading in the case. After the ac- tion is at issue (see Rule 224), it will ordinarily, without any further request by the Court for information as to readiness for submission, be placed on a calendar for submission to the Court. See also Rule 229.

RULE 223. OTHER PLEADINGS

(a) Answer: (1) *Time To Answer or Move:* The Commissioner shall have 30 days from the date of service of the petition within which to file an answer or move with respect to the petition, or, in an action for additional disclosure, to file an election not to defend pursuant to Code section 6110(f)(4)(B), in which event the Commissioner shall be relieved of the obligation of filing an answer or any subsequent pleading. With respect to intervention when the Commissioner elects not to defend, see Rule 225.

(2) *Form and Content:* The answer shall be drawn so that it will advise the petitioner and the Court fully of the nature of the defense. It shall contain a specific admission or denial of each material allegation in the petition. If the Commissioner shall be without knowledge or information sufficient to form a belief as to the truth of an allegation, then the Commissioner shall so state, and such statement shall have the effect of a denial. If the Commissioner intends to qualify or to deny only a part of an allegation, then the Commissioner shall specify so much of it as is true and shall qualify or deny only the remainder. In addition, the answer shall contain a clear and concise statement of every ground, together with the facts in support thereof on which the Commissioner relies and has the burden of proof. Paragraphs of the answer shall be designated to correspond to those of the petition to which they relate.

(3) *Effect of Answer:* Every material allegation set out in the petition and not expressly admitted or denied in the answer shall be deemed to be admitted.

(b) Reply: Each petitioner may file a reply or move with respect to the answer within 20 days from the date of service of the answer. Where a reply is filed, every affirmative allegation set out in the answer and not expressly admitted or denied in the reply, shall be deemed to be admitted. Where a reply is not filed, the affirmative allegations in the answer will be deemed denied. Any new material contained in the reply shall be deemed denied.

RULE 224. JOINDER OF ISSUE

A disclosure action shall be deemed at issue upon the filing of the reply or at the expiration of the time for doing so.

RULE 225. INTERVENTION

(a) Who May Intervene: The persons to whom notice is required to be given by the Commissioner pursuant to Code section 6110(d)(3) or (f)(3)(B) or (4)(B) shall have the right to intervene in the action as to which the notice was given. The Commissioner shall append a copy of the petition to any such notice.

(b) Procedure: If a person desires to intervene, then such person shall file an initial pleading, which shall be a petition in intervention or an answer in intervention, not later than 30 days after mailing by the Commissioner of the notice referred to in paragraph (a) of this Rule. In an action for additional disclosure where the Commissioner elects not to de- fend pursuant to Code section 6110(f)(4)(B), the Commissioner shall mail to each person, to whom the Commissioner has mailed the notice referred to in paragraph (a) of this Rule, a notice of the Commissioner's election not to defend, and any such person desiring to intervene shall have 30 days after such mailing within which to file a petition in intervention or an answer in intervention. The initial pleading of an intervenor, whether a petition or answer, shall show the basis for the right to intervene and shall include, to the ex- tent appropriate, the same elements as are required for a petition under Rule 221 or an answer under Rule 223. An intervenor shall otherwise be subject to the same rules of procedure as apply to other parties. With respect to anonymous intervention, see Rule 227.

RULE 226. JOINDER OF PARTIES

The joinder of parties in a disclosure action shall be subject to the following requirements:

(a) Commencement of Action: Any person who meets the requirements for commencing such an action may join with any other such person in filing a petition with respect to the same written determination, prior written determina- tion, or background file document. But see Code sec. 6110(f)(3)(B), (h)(4).

(b) Consolidation of Actions: If more than one peti- tion is filed with respect to the same written determination, prior written determination, or background file document, then see Rule 141 with respect to the consolidation of the actions.

RULE 227. ANONYMOUS PARTIES

(a) Petitioners: A petitioner in an action to restrain disclosure relating to either a written determination or a prior written determination may file the petition anonymously, if appropriate.

(b) Intervenors: An intervenor may proceed anony- mously, if appropriate, in any disclosure action.

(c) Procedure: A party who proceeds pursuant to this Rule shall be designated as "Anonymous". In all cases where a party proceeds anonymously pursuant to paragraph (a) or (b) of this Rule, such party shall set forth in a separate paper such party's name and address and the reasons why such party seeks to proceed anonymously. Such separate paper shall be filed with such party's initial pleading. Anonymity, where appropriate, shall be preserved to the maximum ex- tent consistent with the proper conduct of the action. See Rule 13(d), relating to contempt of Court. With respect to confidential treatment of pleadings and other papers, see Rule 228.

RULE 228. CONFIDENTIALITY

(a) Confidentiality: The petition and all other papers submitted to the Court in any disclosure action shall be placed and retained by the Court in a confidential file and shall not be open to inspection unless otherwise permitted by the Court.

(b) Publicity of Court Proceedings: On order of the Court portions or all of the hearings, testimony, evidence, and reports in any action under this Title may be closed to the public or to inspection by the public, to the extent deemed by the Court to be appropriate in order to preserve the anonymity, privacy, or confidentiality of any person involved in an action within Code section 6110. See Code sec. 6110(f)(6).

RULE 229. BURDEN OF PROOF

The burden of proof shall be upon the petitioner as to the jurisdictional requirements described in Rule 220(c). As to other matters, the burden of proof shall be determined consistently with Rule 142(a), subject to the following:

(a) In an action for additional disclosure, the burden of proof as to the issue of whether disclosure should be made shall be on the Commissioner and on any other person seek- ing to deny disclosure. See Code sec. 6110(f)(4)(A).

(b) In an action to restrain disclosure, the burden of proof as to the issue of whether disclosure should be made shall be upon the petitioner.

(c) In a third party contact action, the burden of proof shall be on the petitioner to establish that one could reason- ably conclude that an impropriety occurred or undue influ- ence was exercised with respect to the written determination by or on behalf of the person whose identity is sought.

RULE 229A. PROCEDURE IN ACTIONS HEARD BY A SPECIAL TRIAL JUDGE OF THE COURT

(a) Where the Special Trial Judge Is To Make the Decision: If a disclosure action is assigned to a Special Trial Judge who is authorized in the order of assignment to make the decision, then the opinion and proposed decision of the Special Trial Judge shall be submitted to and approved by the Chief Judge, or by another Judge designated by the Chief Judge for that purpose, prior to service of the opinion and decision upon the parties.

(b) Where the Special Trial Judge Is Not To Make the Decision: If a disclosure action is assigned to a Special Trial Judge who is not authorized in the order of assignment to make the decision, then the procedure provided in Rule 183 shall be followed.

TITLE XXIII

CLAIMS FOR LITIGATION AND ADMINISTRATIVE COSTS

RULE 230. GENERAL

(a) Applicability: The Rules of this Title XXIII set forth the special provisions which apply to claims for reason- able litigation and administrative costs authorized by Code section 7430. Except as otherwise provided in this Title, the other Rules of Practice and Procedure of the Court, to the extent pertinent, are applicable to such claims for reasonable litigation and administrative costs. See Title XXVI for Rules relating to separate actions for administrative costs, authorized by Code section 7430(f)(2).

(b) Definitions: As used in the Rules in this Title—

(1) "Reasonable litigation costs" include the items described in Code section 7430(c)(1).

(2) "Reasonable administrative costs" include the items described in Code section 7430(c)(2).

(3) "Court proceeding" means any action brought in this Court in connection with the determination, collection, or refund of tax, interest, or penalty.

(4) "Administrative proceeding" means any procedure or other action within the Internal Revenue Service in connection with the determination, collection, or refund of tax, interest, or penalty.

(5) In the case of a partnership action, the term "party" includes the partner who filed the petition, the tax matters partner, and each person who satisfies the requirements of Code section 6226(c) and (d) or 6228(a)(4). See Rule 247(a).

(6) "Attorney's fees" include fees for the services of an individual (whether or not an attorney) who is authorized to practice before the Court or before the Internal Revenue Service. For the procedure for admission to practice before the Court, see Rule 200.

RULE 231. CLAIMS FOR LITIGATION AND

ADMINISTRATIVE COSTS

(a) **Time and Manner of Claim:** (1) *Agreed Cases:* Where the parties have reached a settlement which disposes of all issues in the case including litigation and administrative costs, an award of reasonable litigation and administrative costs, if any, shall be included in the stipulated decision submitted by the parties for entry by the Court.

(2) *Unagreed Cases:* Where a party has substantially prevailed or is treated as the prevailing party in the case of a qualified offer made as described in Code section 7430(g), and wishes to claim reasonable litigation or administrative costs, and there is no agreement as to that party's entitlement to such costs, a claim shall be made by motion filed—

(A) within 30 days after the service of a written opinion determining the issues in the case;

(B) within 30 days after the service of the pages of the transcript that contain findings of fact or opinion stated orally pursuant to Rule 152 (or a written sum- mary thereof); or

(C) after the parties have settled all issues in the case other than litigation and administrative costs. See paragraphs (b)(3) and (c) of this Rule regarding the filing of a stipulation of settlement with the motion in such cases.

(b) **Content of Motion:** A motion for an award of reasonable litigation or administrative costs shall be in writing and shall contain the following:

(1) A statement that the moving party is a party to a Court proceeding that was commenced after February 28, 1983;

(2) if the claim includes a claim for administrative costs, a statement that the administrative proceeding was commenced after November 10, 1988;

(3) a statement sufficient to demonstrate that the moving party has substantially prevailed with respect to either the amount in controversy or the most significant issue or set of issues presented, or is treated as the prevailing party in the case of a qualified offer made as described in Code section 7430(g), either in the Court proceeding or, if the claim includes a claim for administrative costs, in the administrative proceeding, including a stipulation in the form prescribed by paragraph (c) of this Rule as to any set- tled issues;

(4) (4) a statement that the moving party meets the net worth requirements, if applicable, of section 2412(d)(2)(B) of title 28, United States Code (as in effect on October 22, 1986), which statement shall be supported by an affidavit or a declaration executed by the moving party and not by counsel for the moving party;

(5) a statement that the moving party has exhausted the administrative remedies available to such party within the

Internal Revenue Service;

(6) a statement that the moving party has not unreasonably protracted the Court proceeding and, if the claim includes a claim for administrative costs, the administrative proceeding;

[2](7) a statement of the specific litigation and administrative costs for which the moving party claims an award, supported by an affidavit or a declaration in the form prescribed in paragraph (d) of this Rule;

(8) if the moving party requests a hearing on the mo- tion, a statement of the reasons why the motion cannot be disposed of by the Court without a hearing (see Rule 232(a)(2) regarding the circumstances in which the Court will direct a hearing); and

(9) an appropriate prayer for relief.

(c) **Stipulation as to Settled Issues:** If some or all of the issues in a case (other than litigation and administrative costs) have been settled by the parties, then a motion for an award of reasonable litigation or administrative costs shall be accompanied by a stipulation, signed by the parties or by their counsel, setting forth the terms of the settlement as to each such issue (including the amount of tax involved). A stipulation of settlement shall be binding upon the parties unless otherwise permitted by the Court or agreed upon by those parties.

(d) **Affidavit or Declaration in Support of Costs Claimed:** A motion for an award of reasonable litigation or administrative costs shall be accompanied by a detailed affidavit or declaration by the moving party or counsel for the moving party which sets forth distinctly the nature and amount of each item of costs for which an award is claimed.

(e) **Qualified Offer:** If a qualified offer was made by the moving party as described in Code section 7430(g), then a motion for award of reasonable litigation or administrative costs shall be accompanied by a copy of such offer.

RULE 232. DISPOSITION OF CLAIMS FOR LITIGATION AND ADMINISTRATIVE COSTS

(a) **General:** A motion for reasonable litigation or administrative costs may be disposed of in one or more of the following ways, in the discretion of the Court:

(1) The Court may take action after the Commissioner's written response to the motion is filed. (See paragraph (b)).

(2) After the Commissioner's response is filed, the Court may direct that the moving party file a reply to the Commissioner's response. Additionally, the Court may direct a hearing, which will be held at a location that serves the convenience of the parties and the Court. A motion for reasonable litigation or administrative costs ordinarily will be disposed of without a hearing unless it is clear from the

motion, the Commissioner's written response, and the moving party's reply that there is a bona fide factual dispute that cannot be resolved without an evidentiary hearing.

(b) Response by the Commissioner: The Commissioner shall file a written response within 60 days after service of the motion. The Commissioner's response shall contain the following:

(1) A clear and concise statement of each reason why the Commissioner alleges that the position of the Commissioner in the Court proceeding and, if the claim includes a claim for administrative costs, in the administrative proceeding, was substantially justified, and a statement of the facts on which the Commissioner relies to support each of such reasons;

(2) a statement whether the Commissioner agrees that the moving party has substantially prevailed with respect to either the amount in controversy or the most significant issue or set of issues presented, or is treated as the prevailing party in the case of a qualified offer made as described in Code section 7430(g), either in the Court proceeding or, if the claim includes a claim for administrative costs, in the administrative proceeding.

(3) a statement whether the Commissioner agrees that the moving party meets the net worth requirements, if applicable, as provided by law;

(4) a statement whether the Commissioner agrees that the moving party has exhausted the administrative remedies available to such party within the Internal Revenue Service;

(5) a statement whether the Commissioner agrees that the moving party has not unreasonably protracted the Court proceeding and, if the claim includes a claim for administrative costs, the administrative proceeding;

(6) a statement whether the Commissioner agrees that the amounts of costs claimed are reasonable; and

(7) the basis for the Commissioner's disagreeing with any such allegations by the moving party.

If the Commissioner agrees with the moving party's request for a hearing, or if the Commissioner requests a hearing, then such response shall include a statement of the Commissioner's reasons why the motion cannot be disposed of with- out a hearing.

(c) Conference Required: After the date for filing the Commissioner's written response and prior to the date for filing a reply, if one is required by the Court, counsel for the Commissioner and the moving party or counsel for the moving party shall confer and attempt to reach an agreement as to each of the allegations by the parties. The Court expects that, at such conference, the moving party or counsel for the moving party shall make available to counsel for the Com- missioner substantially the same information relating to any claim for attorney's fees which, in the absence of an agreement, the moving party would be required to file with the Court pursuant to paragraph (d) of this Rule.

[1](d) **Additional Affidavit or Declaration:** Where the Commissioner's response indicates that the Commissioner and the moving party are unable to agree as to the amount of attorney's fees that is reasonable, counsel for the moving party shall, within 30 days after service of the Commissioner's response, file an additional affidavit or declaration which shall include:

(1) A detailed summary of the time expended by each individual for whom fees are sought, including a description of the nature of the services performed during each period of time summarized. Each such individual is expected to maintain contemporaneous, complete, and standardized time records which accurately reflect the work done by such individual. Where the reasonableness of the hours claimed becomes an issue, counsel is expected to make such time records available for inspection by the Court or by counsel for the Commissioner upon request.

(2) The customary fee for the type of work involved. Counsel shall provide specific evidence of the prevailing community rate for the type of work involved as well as specific evidence of counsel's actual billing practice during the time period involved. Counsel may establish the prevailing community rate by affidavits or declarations of other counsel with similar qualifications reciting the precise fees they have received from clients in comparable cases, by evidence of recent fees awarded by the courts or through settlement to counsel of comparable reputation and experience performing similar work, or by reliable legal publications.

(3) A description of the fee arrangement with the client. If any part of the fee is payable only on condition that the Court award such fee, the description shall specifically so state.

(4) The preclusion of other employment by counsel, if any, due to acceptance of the case.

(5) Any time limitations imposed by the client or by the circumstances.

(6) Any other problems resulting from the acceptance of the case.

(7) The professional qualifications and experience of each individual for whom fees are sought.

(8) The nature and length of the professional relationship with the client.

(9) Awards in similar cases, if any.

(10) A statement whether there is a special factor, such as the limited availability of qualified attorneys for the case,

the difficulty of the issues presented in the case, or the local availability of tax expertise, to justify a rate in excess of the rate otherwise permitted for the services of attorneys under Code section 7430(c)(1).

(11) Any other information counsel believes will assist the Court in evaluating counsel's claim, which may include, but shall not be limited to, information relating to the novelty and difficulty of the questions presented, the skill required to perform the legal services properly, and any efforts to settle the case.

Where there are several counsel of record, all of whom are members of or associated with the same firm, an affidavit or a declaration filed by first counsel of record or that counsel's designee (see Rule 21(b)(2)) shall satisfy the requirements of this paragraph, and an affidavit or a declaration by each counsel of record shall not be required.

(e) Burden of Proof: The moving party shall have the burden of proving that the moving party has substantially prevailed or is treated as the prevailing party in the case of a qualified offer made as described in Code section 7430(g); that the moving party has exhausted the administrative remedies available to the moving party within the Internal Revenue Service; that the moving party has not unreasonably protracted the Court proceeding or, if the claim includes a claim for administrative costs, the administrative proceeding; that the moving party meets the net worth requirements, if applicable, as provided by law; that the amount of costs claimed is reasonable; and that the moving party has sub- stantially prevailed with respect to either the amount in controversy or the most significant issue or set of issues presented either in the Court proceeding or, if the claim includes a claim for administrative costs, in the administrative proceeding; except that the moving party shall not be treated as the prevailing party if the Commissioner establishes that the position of the Commissioner was substantially justified. See Code sec. 7430(c)(4)(B).

(f) Disposition: The Court's disposition of a motion for reasonable litigation or administrative costs shall be included in the decision entered in the case. Where the Court in its opinion states that the decision will be entered under Rule 155, or where the parties have settled all of the issues other than litigation and administrative costs, the Court will issue an order granting or denying the motion and determining the amount of reasonable litigation and administrative costs, if any, to be awarded. The parties, or either of them, shall thereafter submit a proposed decision including an award of any such costs, or a denial thereof, for entry by the Court.

RULE 233. MISCELLANEOUS

For provisions prohibiting the inclusion of a claim for reasonable litigation and administrative costs in the petition, see Rule 34(b) (petition in a deficiency or liability action), Rule 211(b) (petition in a declaratory judgment action), Rules 241(c) and 301(c) (petition in a partnership action), Rule 291(c) (petition in an employment status action), Rule 321(b) (petition in an action for determination of relief from joint and several liability on a joint return), and Rule 331(b) (petition in a lien or levy action). For provisions regarding discovery, see Rule 70(a)(2). For provisions prohibiting the introduction of evidence regarding a claim for reasonable litigation or administrative costs at the trial of the case, see Rule 143(a).

TITLE XXIV PARTNERSHIP ACTIONS

RULE 240. GENERAL

(a) Applicability: The Rules of this Title XXIV set forth the special provisions which apply to actions for readjustment of partnership items under Code section 6226 and actions for adjustment of partnership items under Code section 6228. Except as otherwise provided in this Title, the other Rules of Practice and Procedure of the Court, to the extent pertinent, are applicable to such partnership actions.

(b) Definitions: As used in the Rules in this Title—

(1) The term "partnership" means a partnership as defined in Code section 6231(a)(1).

(2) A "partnership action" is either an "action for readjustment of partnership items" under Code section 6226 or an "action for adjustment of partnership items" under Code section 6228.

(3) The term "partnership item" means any item described in Code section 6231(a)(3).

(4) The term "tax matters partner" means the person who is the tax matters partner under Code section 6231(a)(7) and who under these Rules is responsible for keeping each partner fully informed of the partnership ac- tion. See Code secs. 6223(g), 6230(l).

(5) A "notice of final partnership administrative adjustment" is the notice described in Code section 6223(a)(2).

(6) The term "administrative adjustment request" means a request for an administrative adjustment of partnership items filed by the tax matters partner on behalf of the partnership under Code section 6227(c).

(7) The term "partner" means a person who was a partner as defined in Code section 6231(a)(2) at any time during any partnership taxable year at issue in a partnership action.

(8) The term "notice partner" means a person who is a notice partner under Code section 6231(a)(8).

(9) The term "5-percent group" means a 5-percent group as defined in Code section 6231(a)(11).

(c) Jurisdictional Requirements: The Court does not have jurisdiction of a partnership action under this Title unless the following conditions are satisfied:

(1) *Actions for Readjustment of Partnership Items:* (A) The Commissioner has issued a notice of final partnership administrative adjustment. See Code sec. 6226(a) and (b).

(B) A petition for readjustment of partnership items is filed with the Court by the tax matters partner within the period specified in Code section 6226(a), or by a partner other than the tax matters partner subject to the conditions and within the period specified in Code section 6226(b).

(2) *Actions for Adjustment of Partnership Items:* (A) The Commissioner has not allowed all or some of the adjustments requested in an administrative adjustment request. See Code sec. 6228(a).

(B) A petition for adjustment of partnership items is filed with the Court by the tax matters partner subject to the conditions and within the period specified in Code section 6228(a)(2) and (3).

(d) Form and Style of Papers: All papers filed in a partnership action shall be prepared in the form and style set forth in Rule 23, except that the caption shall state the name of the partnership and the full name and surname of any partner filing the petition and shall indicate whether such partner is the tax matters partner, as for example, "ABC Partnership, Mary Doe, Tax Matters Partner, Petitioner" or "ABC Partnership, Richard Roe, A Partner Other Than the Tax Matters Partner, Petitioner".

RULE 241. COMMENCEMENT OF PARTNERSHIP ACTION

[1](a) **Commencement of Action:** A partnership action shall be commenced by filing a petition with the Court. See Rule 20, relating to the commencement of case; the taxpayer identification number to be provided under paragraph (b) of that Rule shall be the employer identification number of the partnership. See also Rule 22, relating to the place and manner of filing the petition; Rule 32, relating to form of pleadings; Rule 34(e), relating to number of copies to be filed; and Rule 240(d), relating to caption of papers.

(b) Content of Petition: Each petition shall be entitled either "Petition for Readjustment of Partnership Items under Code Section 6226" or "Petition for Adjustment of Partnership Items under Code Section 6228". Each such petition shall contain the allegations described in paragraph (c) of this Rule, and the allegations described in paragraph (d)   or (e) of this Rule.

(c)   All Petitions: All petitions in partnership actions   shall contain the following:

(1)   The name and State of legal residence of the petitioner.

(2)   The name and principal place of business of the partnership at the time the petition is filed.

(3)   The city and State of the office of the Internal Revenue Service with which the partnership's return for the period in controversy was filed.

A claim for reasonable litigation or administrative costs shall not be included in the petition in a partnership action. For the requirements as to claims for reasonable litigation or administrative costs, see Rule 231.

(d)   Petition for Readjustment of Partnership Items: In addition to including the information specified in para- graph (c) of this Rule, a petition for readjustment of partner- ship items shall also contain:

(1)   *All Petitions:* All petitions for readjustment of partnership items shall contain:

(A)   The date of the notice of final partnership administrative adjustment and the city and State of the office   of the Internal Revenue Service which issued the notice.

(B)   The year or years or other periods for which the notice of final partnership administrative adjustment was issued.

(C)   Clear and concise statements of each and every error which the petitioner alleges to have been committed by the Commissioner in the notice of final partnership administrative adjustment. The assignments of error shall include issues in respect of which the burden of proof is on the Commissioner. Any issues not raised   in the assignments of error, or in the assignments of error in any amendment to the petition, shall be deemed to be conceded. Each assignment of error shall be set forth in a separately lettered subparagraph.

(D)   Clear and concise lettered statements of the facts on which the petitioner bases the assignments of error, except with respect to those assignments of error as to which the burden of proof is on the Commissioner.

(E)   A prayer setting forth relief sought by the petitioner.

(F)   The signature, mailing address, and telephone number of each petitioner or each petitioner's counsel, as well as counsel's Tax Court bar number.

(G)   A copy of the notice of final partnership administrative adjustment, which shall be appended to the petition, and with which there shall be included so much of any statement accompanying the notice as is material to the issues raised by the assignments of error. If the notice of final partnership administrative adjustment or any accompanying statement incorporates by reference any prior notices, or other material furnished by the Internal Revenue Service, such parts thereof as are material to the assignments of error likewise shall be appended to the petition.

(2) *Petitions by Tax Matters Partner:* In addition to including the information specified in paragraph (d)(1) of this Rule, a petition filed by a tax matters partner shall also contain a separate numbered paragraph stating that the pleader is the tax matters partner.

(3) *Petitions by Other Partners:* In addition to including the information specified in paragraph (d)(1) of this Rule, a petition filed by a partner other than the tax matters partner shall also contain:

(A) A separate numbered paragraph stating that the pleader is a notice partner or a representative of a 5-percent group. See Code sec. 6226(b)(1).

(B) A separate numbered paragraph setting forth facts establishing that the pleader satisfies the requirements of Code section 6226(d).

(C) A separate numbered paragraph stating the name and current address of the tax matters partner.

(D) A separate numbered paragraph stating that the tax matters partner has not filed a petition for readjustment of partnership items within the period specified in Code section 6226(a).

(e) Petition for Adjustment of Partnership Items: In addition to including the information specified in paragraph (c) of this Rule, a petition for adjustment of partnership items shall also contain:

(1) A statement that the petitioner is the tax matters partner.

(2) The date that the administrative adjustment request was filed and other proper allegations showing jurisdiction in the Court in accordance with the requirements of Code section 6228(a)(1) and (2).

(3) The year or years or other periods to which the administrative adjustment request relates.

(4) The city and State of the office of the Internal Revenue Service with which the administrative adjustment request was filed.

(5) A clear and concise statement describing each partnership item on the partnership return that is sought to be changed, and the basis for each such requested change. Each such statement shall be set forth in a separately lettered subparagraph.

(6) Clear and concise lettered statements of the facts on which the petitioner relies in support of such requested

changes in treatment of partnership items.

(7)   A prayer setting forth relief sought by the petitioner.

(8)   The signature, mailing address, and telephone number of the petitioner or the petitioner's counsel, as well as counsel's Tax Court bar number.

(9)   A copy of the administrative adjustment request shall be appended to the petition.

(f) Notice of Filing: (1) *Petitions by Tax Matters Partner:* After receiving the Notification of Receipt of Petition from the Court and within 30 days after filing the petition,   the tax matters partner shall serve notice of the filing of the petition on each partner in the partnership as required   by   Code section 6223(g). Said notice shall include the docket number assigned to the case by the Court (see Rule 35) and the date the petition was served by the Clerk on the Com- missioner.

(2) *Petitions by Other Partners:* Within 5 days after re- ceiving the Notification of Receipt of Petition from the Court, the petitioner shall serve a copy of the petition on   the tax matters partner, and at the same time notify the tax matters partner of the docket number assigned to the case by the Court (see Rule 35) and the date the petition was served by the Clerk on the Commissioner. Within 30   days after receiving a copy of the petition and the afore- mentioned notification from the petitioner, the tax matters partner shall serve notice of the filing of the petition on each partner in the partnership as required by Code sec- tion 6223(g). Said notice shall include the docket number assigned to the case by the Court and the date the petition was served by the Clerk on the Commissioner.

(g)   Copy of Petition To Be Provided All Partners: Upon request by any partner in the partnership as referred   to in Code section 6231(a)(2)(A), the tax matters partner   shall, within 10 days of receipt of such request, make avail- able to such partner a copy of any petition filed by the tax matters partner or by any other partner.

(h)   Joinder   of   Parties: (1)   *Permissive   Joinder:*   A separate petition shall be filed with respect to each notice of final partnership administrative adjustment or each adminis- trative adjustment request issued to separate partnerships. However, a single petition for readjustment of partnership items or petition for adjustment of partnership items may be filed seeking readjustments or adjustments of partnership items with respect to more than one notice of final partner- ship administrative adjustment or administrative adjustment request if the notices or requests pertain to the same part- nership. For the procedures to be followed by partners who wish to intervene or participate in a partnership action, see Rule 245.

(2) *Severance or Other Orders:* With respect to a case based upon multiple notices of final partnership adminis-

trative adjustment or administrative adjustment requests, the Court may order a severance and a separate case to be maintained with respect to one or more of such notices or requests whenever it appears to the Court that proceeding separately is in furtherance of convenience, or to avoid prejudice, or when separate trials will be conducive to expedition or economy.

RULE 242. REQUEST FOR PLACE OF TRIAL

At the time of filing a petition in a partnership action, a request for place of trial shall be filed in accordance with Rule 140.

RULE 243. OTHER PLEADINGS

(a) Answer: The Commissioner shall file an answer or shall move with respect to the petition within the periods specified in and in accordance with the provisions of Rule 36.

(b) Reply: For provisions relating to the filing of a reply, see Rule 37.

RULE 244. JOINDER OF ISSUE IN PARTNERSHIP ACTION

A partnership action shall be deemed at issue upon the later of:

(1)   The time provided by Rule 38, or

(2)   the expiration of the period within which a notice of election to intervene or to participate may be filed under Rule 245(a) or (b).

RULE 245. INTERVENTION AND PARTICIPATION

(a) Tax Matters Partner: The tax matters partner may intervene in an action for readjustment of partnership items brought by another partner or partners by filing a no- tice of election to intervene with the Court. Such notice shall state that the intervenor is the tax matters partner and shall   be filed within 90 days from the date of service of the petition by the Clerk on the Commissioner. See Code sec. 6226(b)(2); Rule 241(d)(3).

(b) Other Partners: Any other partner who satisfies the requirements of Code section 6226(d) or 6228(a)(4)(B) may participate in the action by filing a notice of election to participate with the Court. Such notice shall set forth facts establishing that such partner satisfies the requirements of Code section 6226(d) in the case of an action for readjustment of partnership items or Code section 6228(a)(4)(B) in the case of an action for adjustment of partnership items and shall be filed within 90 days from the date of service of the petition by the Clerk on the Commissioner. A single notice may be filed by two or more partners; however, each such partner must satisfy all requirements of this paragraph in order for the notice to be treated as filed by or for that partner.

(c) Enlargement of Time: The Court may grant leave to file a notice of election to intervene or a notice of election to participate out of time upon a showing of sufficient cause.

(d) Pleading: No assignment of error, allegation of fact, or other statement in the nature of a pleading shall be included in a notice of election to intervene or notice of election to participate. As to the form and content of a notice of election to intervene and a notice of election to participate, see Appendix I, Forms 11 and 12, respectively.

(e) Amendments to the Petition: A party other than the petitioner who is authorized to raise issues not raised in the petition may do so by filing an amendment to the petition. Such an amendment may be filed, without leave of Court, at any time within the period specified in Rule 245(b). Otherwise, such an amendment may be filed only by leave of Court. See Rule 36(a) for time for responding to amendments to the petition.

RULE 246. SERVICE OF PAPERS

(a) Petitions: All petitions shall be served by the Clerk on the Commissioner.

(b) Papers Issued by the Court: All papers issued by the Court shall be served by the Clerk on the Commissioner, the tax matters partner (whether or not the tax matters partner is a participating partner), and all other participating partners.

(c) All Other Papers: All other papers required to be served (see Rule 21(a)) shall be served by the parties filing such papers. Whenever a paper (other than a petition) is required by these Rules to be filed with the Court, the original paper shall be filed with the Court with certificates by the filing party or the filing party's counsel that service of the paper has been made on each of the other parties set forth in paragraph (b) of this Rule or on such other parties' counsel. The Court may return without filing documents that are not accompanied by certificates of service required by this Rule.

RULE 248   (7/6/12)   169

RULE 247. PARTIES

(a) In General: For purposes of this title of these Rules, the Commissioner, the partner who filed the petition, the tax matters partner, and each person who satisfies the requirements of Code section 6226(c) and (d) or 6228(a)(4) shall be treated as parties to the action.

(b) Participating Partners: Participating partners are the partner who filed the petition and such other partners who have filed either a notice of election to intervene or a no- tice of election to participate in accordance with the provisions of Rule 245. See Code secs. 6226(c), 6228(a)(4)(A).

RULE 248. SETTLEMENT AGREEMENTS

(a) Consent by the Tax Matters Partner to Entry of Decision: A stipulation consenting to entry of decision executed by the tax matters partner and filed with the Court shall bind all parties. The signature of the tax matters part- ner constitutes a certificate by the tax matters partner that no party objects to entry of decision. See Rule 251.

(b) Settlement or Consistent Agreements Entered Into by All Participating Partners or No Objection by Participating Partners:

(1) After the expiration of the time within which to file a notice of election to intervene or to participate under Rule 245(a) or (b), the Commissioner shall move for entry of decision, and shall submit a proposed form of decision with such motion, if—

(A) all of the participating partners have entered into a settlement agreement or consistent agreement with the Commissioner, or all of such partners do not object to the granting of the Commissioner's motion for entry of decision, and

(B) the tax matters partner (if a participating partner) agrees to the proposed decision in the case but does not certify that no party objects to the granting of the Commissioner's motion for entry of decision.

(2) Within 3 days from the date on which the Commissioner's motion for entry of decision is filed with the Court, the Commissioner shall serve on the tax matters partner a certificate showing the date on which the Commissioner's motion was filed with the Court.

(3) Within 3 days after receiving the Commissioner's certificate, the tax matters partner shall serve on all other parties to the action other than the participating partners, a copy of the Commissioner's motion for entry of decision, a copy of the proposed decision, a copy of the Commissioner's certificate showing the date on which the Commissioner's motion was filed with the Court, and a copy of this Rule.

(4) If any party objects to the granting of the Commissioner's motion for entry of decision, then that party shall, within 60 days from the date on which the Commissioner's motion was filed with the Court, file a motion for leave to file a notice of election to intervene or to participate, accompanied by a separate notice of election to intervene or a separate notice of election to participate, as the case may be.

138

If no such motion is filed with the Court within such period, or if the Court should deny such motion, then the Court may enter the proposed decision as its decision in the partnership action. See Code secs. 6226(f), 6228(a)(5); see also Rule 245, relating to intervention and participa- tion, and Rule 251, relating to decisions.

(c) Other Settlement and Consistent Agreements: If a settlement agreement or consistent agreement is not within the scope of paragraph (b) of this Rule, then—

(1) in the case of a participating partner, the Commissioner shall promptly file with the Court a notice of settlement agreement or notice of consistent agreement, whichever may be appropriate, that identifies the participating partner or partners who have entered into the settlement agreement or consistent agreement; and

(2) in the case of any partner who enters into a settlement agreement, the Commissioner shall, within 7 days after the settlement agreement is executed by both the partner and the Commissioner, serve on the tax matters partner a statement which sets forth—

(A) the identity of the party or parties to the settle- ment agreement and the date of the agreement;

(B) the year or years to which the settlement agreement relates; and

(C) the terms of the settlement as to each partnership item and the allocation of such items among the partners. Within 7 days after receiving the statement required by this subparagraph, the tax matters partner shall serve on all par- ties to the action a copy of such statement.

RULE 249. ACTION FOR ADJUSTMENT OF PARTNERSHIP ITEMS TREATED AS ACTION FOR READJUSTMENT OF PARTNERSHIP ITEMS

(a) Amendment to Petition: If, after the filing of a petition for adjustment of partnership items (see Code section 6228(a) and Rule 241(a)) but before the hearing of such petition, the Commissioner mails to the tax matters partner a notice of final partnership administrative adjustment for the partnership taxable year to which the petition relates, then such petition shall be treated as a petition in an action for readjustment of the partnership items to which such notice relates. The petitioner, within 90 days after the date on which the notice of final partnership administrative adjust- ment is mailed to the tax matters partner, shall file an amendment to the petition, setting forth every error which the petitioner alleges to have been committed by the Com- missioner in the notice of final partnership administrative adjustment, and the facts on which the petitioner bases the assignments of error. A copy of the notice of final partnership administrative adjustment shall be appended to the amend- ment to the petition. On or before the day the amendment to petition is delivered to the Court, or, if the amendment to petition is mailed to the Court, on or before the day of mail- ing, the tax matters partner shall serve notice of the filing of the amendment to petition on each partner in the partner- ship as required by Code section 6223(g).

(b) Participation: Any partner who has filed a timely notice of election to participate in the action for adjustment of partnership items shall be deemed to have elected to par- ticipate in the action for readjustment of partnership items and need not file another notice of election to do so. Any other partner may participate in the action by filing a notice of election to participate within 90 days from the date of fil- ing of the amendment to petition. See Rule 245.

RULE 250. APPOINTMENT AND REMOVAL OF THE TAX MATTERS PARTNER

(a) Appointment of Tax Matters Partner: If, at the time of commencement of a partnership action by a partner other than the tax matters partner, the tax matters partner is not identified in the petition, then the Court will take such action as may be necessary to establish the identity of the tax matters partner or to effect the appointment of a tax matters partner.

(b) Removal of Tax Matters Partner: After notice and opportunity to be heard, (1) the Court may for cause re- move a partner as the tax matters partner and (2) if the tax matters partner is removed by the Court, or if a partner's status as the tax matters partner is terminated for reason other than removal by the Court, then the Court may ap- point another partner as the tax matters partner if the part- nership fails to designate a successor tax matters partner within such period as the Court may direct.

RULE 251. DECISIONS

A decision entered by the Court in a partnership action shall be binding on all parties. For the definition of parties, see Rule 247(a).

TITLE XXV SUPPLEMENTAL PROCEEDINGS

RULE 260. PROCEEDING TO ENFORCE OVERPAYMENT DETERMINATION

(a) Commencement of Proceeding: (1) *How Pro- ceeding Is Commenced:* A proceeding to enforce an overpay- ment determined by the Court under Code section 6512(b)(1) shall be commenced by filing a motion with the Court. The petitioner shall place on the motion the same docket number as that of the action in which the Court determined the over-payment.

(2) *When Proceeding May Be Commenced:* A proceeding under this Rule may not be commenced before the expiration of 120 days after the decision of the Court determining the overpayment has become final within the meaning of Code section 7481(a).

(b) Content of Motion: A motion to enforce an overpayment determination filed pursuant to this Rule shall contain the following:

(1) The petitioner's name and current mailing address.

(2) A statement whether any dispute exists between the parties regarding either the fact or amount of interest payable in respect of the overpayment determined by the Court and, if such a dispute exists, clear and concise let- tered statements of the facts regarding the dispute and the petitioner's position in respect of each disputed matter.

(3) A copy of the Court's decision which determined the overpayment, together with a copy of any stipulation referred to therein and any computation filed pursuant to Rule 155 setting forth the amount and date of each pay- ment made by the petitioner.

(4) A copy of the petitioner's written demand on the Commissioner to refund the overpayment determined by the Court, together with interest as provided by law; this demand shall have been made not less than 60 days before the filing of the motion under this Rule and shall have been made on the Commissioner through the Commis- sioner's last counsel of record in the action in which the Court determined the overpayment which the petitioner now seeks to enforce by this motion.

(5) If the petitioner requests an evidentiary or other hearing on the motion, then a statement of the reasons why the motion cannot be disposed of by the Court without a hearing. For the circumstances under which the Court will direct a hearing, see paragraph (d) of this Rule.

(c) Response by the Commissioner: Within 30 days after service of a motion filed pursuant to this Rule, the Commissioner shall file a written response. The response shall specifically admit or deny each allegation set forth in the petitioner's motion. If a dispute exists between the par- ties regarding either the fact or amount of interest payable in respect of the overpayment determined by the Court, then the Commissioner's response shall also include clear and con- cise statements of the facts regarding the dispute and the Commissioner's position in respect of each disputed matter. If the Commissioner agrees with the petitioner's request for a hearing, or if the Commissioner requests a hearing, then the response shall include a statement of the Commissioner's reasons why the motion cannot be disposed of without a hearing. If the Commissioner opposes the petitioner's request for a hearing, then the response shall include a statement of the reasons why no hearing is required.

(d) Disposition of Motion: A motion to enforce an overpayment determination filed pursuant to this Rule will ordinarily be disposed of without an evidentiary or other hearing unless it is clear from the motion and the Commissioner's written response that there is a bona fide factual dispute that cannot be resolved without an evidentiary hearing.

(e) Recognition of Counsel: Counsel recognized by the Court in the action in which the Court determined the overpayment which the petitioner now seeks to enforce will be recognized in a proceeding commenced under this Rule. Counsel not so recognized must file an entry of appearance pursuant to Rule 24(a)(3) or a substitution of counsel pursu- ant to Rule 24(d).

(f) Cross-Reference: For the need, in the case of an overpayment, to include the amount and date of each payment made by the petitioner in any computation for entry of decision, see paragraphs (a) and (b) of Rule 155.

RULE 261. PROCEEDING TO REDETERMINE INTEREST

(a) Commencement of Proceeding: (1) *How Proceeding Is Commenced:* A proceeding to redetermine inter- est on a deficiency assessed under Code section 6215 or to re- determine interest on an overpayment determined under Code section 6512(b) shall be commenced by filing a motion with the Court. The petitioner shall place on the motion the same docket number as that of the action in which the Court redetermined the deficiency or determined the overpayment.

(2) *When Proceeding May Be Commenced:* Any proceeding under this Rule must be commenced within 1 year after the date that the Court's decision becomes final with- in the meaning of Code section 7481(a).

(b) Content of Motion: A motion to redetermine interest filed pursuant to this Rule shall contain:

(1) *All Motions:* All motions to redetermine interest shall contain the following:

(A) The petitioner's name and current mailing address.

(B) A statement setting forth the petitioner's contentions regarding the correct amount of interest, together with a schedule detailing the computation of that amount.

(C) A statement whether the petitioner has discussed the dispute over interest with the Commissioner, and if so, the contentions made by the petitioner; and if not, the reason or reasons why not.

(2) *Motions To Redetermine Interest on a Deficiency:* In addition to including the information described in para-graph (b)(1) of this Rule, a motion to redetermine interest on a deficiency shall also contain:

(A)   A statement that the petitioner has paid the en-tire amount of the deficiency assessed under Code sec-tion 6215 plus interest claimed by the Commissioner in respect of which the proceeding under this Rule has been commenced.

(B)   A schedule setting forth—

(i)   the amount of each payment made by the peti-tioner in respect of the deficiency and interest de-scribed in paragraph (b)(2)(A) of this Rule,

(ii)   the date of each such payment, and

(iii)   if applicable, the part of each such payment al-located by the petitioner to tax and the part of each such payment allocated by the petitioner to interest.

(iv)   A copy of the Court's decision which redeter-mined the deficiency, together with a copy of any no-tice of assessment including any supporting schedules or any collection notice that the petitioner may have received from the Commissioner, in respect of which the proceeding under this Rule has been commenced.

(3) *Motions To Redetermine Interest on an Overpay-ment:* In addition to including the information described in paragraph (b)(1) of this Rule, a motion to redetermine in-terest on an overpayment shall also contain:

(A)   A statement that the Court has determined under Code section 6512(b) that the petitioner has made an overpayment.

(B)   A schedule setting forth—

(i)   the amount and date of each payment made by the petitioner in respect of which the overpayment was determined, and

(ii)   the amount and date of each credit, offset, or refund received from the Commissioner in respect of the overpayment and interest claimed by the peti-tioner.

(C)   A copy of the Court's decision which determined the overpayment, together with a copy of any notice of credit or offset or other correspondence that the peti-tioner may have received from the Commissioner, in re-spect of which the proceeding under this Rule has been commenced.

(4)   If the petitioner requests an evidentiary or other hearing on the motion, then a statement of the reasons why the motion cannot be disposed of by the Court without a hearing. For the circumstances under which the Court will direct a hearing, see paragraph (d) of this Rule.

(c)   Response by the Commissioner: Within 60 days after

143

service of a motion filed pursuant to this Rule, the Commissioner shall file a written response. The response shall specifically address each of the contentions made by the petitioner regarding the correct amount of interest and the petitioner's computation of that amount. The Commissioner shall attach to the Commissioner's response a schedule detailing the computation of interest claimed to be owed to or due from the Commissioner and, in the case of a motion to redetermine interest on an overpayment, the amount and date of each credit, offset, or refund made by the Commissioner and, if applicable, the part of each such credit, offset, or refund allocated by the Commissioner to the overpayment and the part of each such credit, offset, or refund allocated by the Commissioner to interest. If the Commissioner agrees with the petitioner's request for a hearing, or if the Commissioner requests a hearing, then the response shall include a statement of the Commissioner's reasons why the motion cannot be disposed of without a hearing. If the Commissioner opposes the petitioner's request for a hearing, then the response shall include a statement of the reasons why no hearing is required.

(d) Disposition of Motion: A motion to redetermine interest filed pursuant to this Rule will ordinarily be disposed of without an evidentiary or other hearing unless it is clear from the motion and the Commissioner's written response that there is a bona fide factual dispute that cannot be resolved without an evidentiary hearing.

(e) Recognition of Counsel: Counsel recognized by the Court in the action in which the Court redetermined the deficiency or determined the overpayment the interest in respect of which the petitioner now seeks a redetermination will be recognized in a proceeding commenced under this Rule. Counsel not so recognized must file an entry of appearance pursuant to Rule 24(a)(3) or a substitution of counsel pursuant to Rule 24(d).

RULE 262. PROCEEDING TO MODIFY DECISION IN ESTATE TAX CASE INVOLVING SECTION 6166 ELECTION

(a) Commencement of Proceeding: A proceeding to modify a decision in an estate tax case pursuant to Code section 7481(d) shall be commenced by filing a motion with the Court accompanied by a proposed form of decision. The petitioner shall place on the motion and the proposed form of decision the same docket number as that of the action in which the Court entered the decision which the petitioner now seeks to modify.

(b) Content of Motion: A motion to modify a decision filed pursuant to this Rule shall contain the following:

(1) The name and current mailing address of each fiduciary authorized to act on behalf of the estate.

(2) A copy of the decision entered by the Court which the petitioner now seeks to modify.

(3) A statement that the time for payment by the estate of an amount of tax imposed by Code section 2001 has been extended pursuant to Code section 6166.

(4) A schedule setting forth—

(A) the amount of interest paid by the estate on any portion of the tax imposed by Code section 2001 on the estate for which the time of payment has been extended under Code section 6166;

(B) the amount of interest on any estate, succession, legacy, or inheritance tax imposed by a State on the es- tate during the period of the extension of time for pay- ment under Code section 6166; and

(C) the date that each such amount of interest was paid by the estate.

(5) A statement describing the nature of any dispute within the purview of Code section 7481(d), or if no such dispute exists, then a statement to that effect.

(6) If the petitioner requests an evidentiary or other hearing on the motion, then a statement of the reasons why the motion cannot be disposed of by the Court without a hearing. For the circumstances under which the Court will direct a hearing, see paragraph (d) of this Rule.

(c) Response by Commissioner in Unagreed Case: If a dispute exists between the parties regarding either the petitioner's right to relief under Code section 7481(d) or the amount of interest deductible as an administrative expense under Code section 2053, then the Commissioner shall, with-in 60 days after service of a motion filed pursuant to this Rule, file a written response accompanied by a proposed form of decision. The response shall identify the nature of the dis- pute, shall specifically admit or deny each allegation set forth in the petitioner's motion, and shall state the Commissioner's position in respect of each disputed matter. If the Commis-sioner agrees with the petitioner's request for a hearing, or if the Commissioner requests a hearing, then the response shall include a statement of the Commissioner's reasons why the motion cannot be disposed of without a hearing. If the Commissioner opposes the petitioner's request for a hearing, then the response shall include a statement of the reasons why no hearing is required.

(d) Disposition of Motion: A motion to modify a deci-sion filed pursuant to this Rule will ordinarily be disposed of without an evidentiary or other hearing unless it is clear from the motion and the Commissioner's written response that there is a bona fide factual dispute that cannot be re- solved without an evidentiary hearing.

(e) Recognition of Counsel: Counsel recognized by the Court in the action in which the Court entered the deci- sion which the petitioner now seeks to modify will be recog- nized in a proceeding commenced under this Rule. Counsel not so recognized must file an entry of appearance pursuant to Rule 24(a)(3) or a substitution of counsel pursuant to Rule 24(d).

(f) **Cross-Reference:** For the need to move the Court to retain its official case file in the action with respect to which the petitioner seeks to modify the decision, see Rule 157.

TITLE XXVI ACTIONS FOR ADMINISTRATIVE COSTS

RULE 270. GENERAL

(a) **Applicability:** The Rules of this Title XXVI set forth the special provisions which apply to actions for admin- istrative costs under Code section 7430(f)(2). Except as other- wise provided in this Title, the other Rules of Practice and Procedure of the Court, to the extent pertinent, are applica- ble to such actions for administrative costs.

(b) **Definitions:** As used in the Rules in this Title—

(1) "Reasonable administrative costs" means the items described in Code section 7430(c)(2).

(2) "Attorney's fees" include fees for the services of an individual (whether or not an attorney) admitted to prac- tice before the Court or authorized to practice before the Internal Revenue Service. For the procedure for admission to practice before the Court, see Rule 200.

(3) "Administrative proceeding" means any procedure or other action within the Internal Revenue Service in con- nection with the determination, collection, or refund of any tax, interest, or penalty.

(c) **Jurisdictional Requirements:** The Court does not have jurisdiction of an action for administrative costs under this Title unless the following conditions are satisfied:

(1) The Commissioner has made a decision denying (in whole or in part) an award for reasonable administrative costs under Code section 7430(a).

(2) A petition for an award for reasonable administra- tive costs is filed with the Court within the period specified in Code section 7430(f)(2).

(d) **Burden of Proof:** For the rules regarding the bur- den of proof in claims for administrative costs, see Rule 232(e).

RULE 271. COMMENCEMENT OF ACTION FOR ADMINISTRATIVE COSTS

(a) **Commencement of Action:** An action for an award for reasonable administrative costs under Code section 7430(f)(2) shall be commenced by filing a petition with the Court. See Rule 20, relating to commencement of case; Rule

22, relating to the place and manner of filing the petition;   and Rule 32, relating to the form of pleadings.

(b)   Content of Petition: A petition filed pursuant to this Rule shall be entitled "Petition for Administrative Costs (Sec. 7430(f)(2))". Such a petition shall be substantially in accordance with Form 3 shown in Appendix I, or shall, in the alternative, contain the following:

(1)   In the case of a petitioner who is an individual, the petitioner's name and State of legal residence; in the case of a petitioner other than an individual, the petitioner's name and principal place of business or principal office or agency; and, in all cases, the petitioner's mailing address.   The mailing address, State of legal residence, principal place of business, or principal office or agency, shall be stated as of the date that the petition is filed.

(2)   The date of the decision denying an award for administrative costs in respect of which the petition is filed, and the city and State of the office of the Internal Revenue Service which issued the decision.

(3)   The amount of administrative costs claimed by the petitioner in the administrative proceeding; the amount of administrative costs denied by the Commissioner; and, if different from the amount denied, the amount of administrative costs now claimed by the petitioner.

(4)   Clear and concise lettered statements of the facts on which the petitioner relies to establish that, in the administrative proceeding, the petitioner substantially prevailed with respect to either the amount in controversy or the most significant issue or set of issues presented in the administrative proceeding.

(5)   A statement that the petitioner meets the net worth requirements of section 2412(d)(2)(B) of title 28, United States Code (as in effect on October 22, 1986).

(6)   The signature, mailing address, and telephone number of each petitioner or each petitioner's counsel, as well as counsel's Tax Court bar number.

(7)   A copy of the decision denying (in whole or in part) an award for reasonable administrative costs in respect of which the petition is filed.

(8)   **(c) Filing Fee:** The fee for filing a petition for administrative costs shall be $60, payable at the time of filing. The payment of any fee under this paragraph may be waived if the petitioner establishes to the satisfaction of the Court by an affidavit or a declaration containing specific financial information that the petitioner is unable to make such payment.

RULE 272. OTHER PLEADINGS

(a)   Answer: (1) *General:* The Commissioner shall file an answer or shall move with respect to the petition within the periods specified in and in accordance with the provisions of Rule 36.

(2) *Additional Requirement for Answer:* In addition to the specific admission or denial of each material allegation in the petition, the answer shall contain the following:

(A) Clear and concise lettered statements of the facts on which the Commissioner relies to establish that, in the administrative proceeding, the Commissioner's posi- tion was substantially justified;

(B) a statement whether the Commissioner agrees that the petitioner substantially prevailed in the admin- istrative proceeding with respect to either the amount in controversy or the most significant issue or set of issues presented in the administrative proceeding;

(C) a statement whether the Commissioner agrees that the amount of administrative costs claimed by the petitioner is reasonable;

(D) a statement whether the Commissioner agrees that the petitioner meets the net worth requirements as provided by law; and

(E) the basis for the Commissioner's disagreement with any such allegations by the petitioner.

(3) *Effect of Answer:* Every material allegation set forth in the petition and not expressly admitted or denied in the answer shall be deemed to be admitted. The failure to include in the answer any statement required by sub- paragraph (2) of this paragraph shall be deemed to con- stitute a concession by the Commissioner of that matter.

(b) Reply: A reply to the answer shall not be filed in an action for administrative costs unless the Court, on its own motion or upon motion of the Commissioner, shall otherwise direct. Any reply shall conform to the requirements of Rule 37(b). In the absence of a requirement of a reply, the provi- sions of the second sentence of Rule 37(c) shall not apply and the material allegations of the answer will be deemed denied.

RULE 273. JOINDER OF ISSUE IN ACTION FOR ADMINISTRATIVE COSTS

An action for administrative costs shall be deemed at issue upon the filing of the answer.

RULE 274. APPLICABLE SMALL TAX CASE RULES [1]

Proceedings in an action for administrative costs shall be governed by the provisions of the following Small Tax Case Rules (see Rule 170) with respect to the matters to which they apply: Rule 172 (representation) and Rule 174 (trial).

TITLE XXVII ACTIONS FOR REVIEW OF FAILURE TO ABATE INTEREST

RULE 280. GENERAL

(a) Applicability: The Rules of this Title XXVII set forth the provisions which apply to actions for review of the Commissioner's failure to abate interest under Code section 6404. Except as otherwise provided in this Title, the other Rules of Practice and Procedure of the Court, to the extent pertinent, are applicable to such actions for review.

(b) Jurisdiction: The Court shall have jurisdiction of an action for review of the Commissioner's failure to abate interest under this Title when the following conditions are satisfied:

(1) The Commissioner has mailed a notice of final determination not to abate interest under Code section 6404.

(2) A petition for review of the Commissioner's failure to abate interest is filed with the Court within the period specified in Code section 6404(h) by a taxpayer who meets the requirements of Code section 7430(c)(4)(A)(ii).

RULE 281. COMMENCEMENT OF ACTION FOR REVIEW OF FAILURE TO ABATE INTEREST

(a) Commencement of Action: An action for review of the Commissioner's failure to abate interest under Code sec- tion 6404 shall be commenced by filing a petition with the Court. See Rule 20, relating to the commencement of a case; Rule 22, relating to the place and manner of filing the peti- tion; and Rule 32, regarding the form of pleadings.

(b) Content of Petition: A petition filed pursuant to this Rule shall be entitled ''Petition for Review of Failure To Abate Interest Under Code Section 6404'' and shall contain the following:

(1) In the case of a petitioner who is an individual, the petitioner's name and State of legal residence; in the case of a petitioner other than an individual, the petitioner's name and principal place of business or principal office or agency; and, in all cases, the petitioner's mailing address. The mailing address, State of legal residence, and principal place of business, or principal office or agency, shall be stated as of the date that the petition is filed.

(2) The date of the notice of final determination not to abate interest and the city and State of the office of the In- ternal Revenue Service which issued the notice.

(3) The year or years or other periods to which the fail- ure to abate interest relates.

(4) Clear and concise lettered statements of the facts on which the petitioner relies to establish that the Commis- sioner's final determination not to abate interest was an

abuse of discretion.

(5) A statement that the petitioner meets the require-ments of Code section 7430(c)(4)(A)(ii).

(6) The signature, mailing address, and telephone num-ber of each petitioner or each petitioner's counsel, as well as counsel's Tax Court bar number.

(7) As an attachment, a copy of the notice of final deter-mination denying (in whole or in part) the requested abate-ment.

[1](c) **Filing Fee:** The fee for filing a petition for review of failure to abate interest shall be $60, payable at the time of filing. The payment of any fee under this paragraph may be waived if the petitioner establishes to the satisfaction of the Court by an affidavit or a declaration containing specific financial information that the petitioner is unable to make such payment.

RULE 282. REQUEST FOR PLACE OF TRIAL

At the time of filing a petition for review of failure to abate interest, a request for place of trial shall be filed in accord- ance with Rule 140.

RULE 283. OTHER PLEADINGS

(a) Answer: The Commissioner shall file an answer or shall move with respect to the petition within the periods specified in and in accordance with the provisions of Rule 36.

(b) Reply: For provisions relating to the filing of a reply,

RULE 284. JOINDER OF ISSUE IN ACTION FOR REVIEW OF FAILURE TO ABATE INTEREST

An action for review of the Commissioner's failure to abate interest under Code section 6404 shall be deemed at issue as provided by Rule 38.

TITLE XXVIII ACTIONS FOR REDETERMINATION OF EMPLOYMENT STATUS

RULE 290. GENERAL

(a) Applicability: The Rules of this Title XXVIII set forth the provisions which apply to actions for redetermination of employment status under Code section 7436. Except as otherwise provided in this Title, the other Rules of Practice and Procedure of the Court, to the extent pertinent, are applicable to such actions for redetermination.

(b) Jurisdiction: The Court shall have jurisdiction of an action for redetermination of employment status under this Title when the following conditions are satisfied:

(1)   In connection with an audit of any person, there is an actual controversy involving a determination by the Commissioner as part of an examination that:

(A)   One or more individuals performing services for such person are employees of such person for purposes of subtitle C of the Code, or

(B)   such person is not entitled to the treatment under subsection (a) of sec. 530 of the Revenue Act of 1978, Pub. L. 95–600, 92 Stat. 2885, with respect to such an individual.

(2)   A petition for redetermination of employment status is filed with the Court in accordance with Rule 291 by the person for whom the services are performed.

(c)   Time for Filing After Notice Sent: If the Commissioner sends by certified or registered mail to the petitioner notice of the Commissioner's determination of matters set forth in Code section 7436(a)(1) and (2), then no proceeding may be initiated with respect to such determination unless the petition is filed within the period specified in Code sec- tion 7436(b)(2).

RULE 291. COMMENCEMENT OF ACTION FOR REDETERMINATION OF EMPLOYMENT STATUS

(a)   Commencement of Action: An action for redetermination of employment status under Code section 7436 shall be commenced by filing a petition with the Court. See

Rule 20, relating to the commencement of a case; Rule 22, relating to the place and manner of filing the petition; and Rule 32, relating to the form of pleadings.

(b)   Content of Petition: A petition filed pursuant to this Rule shall be entitled "Petition for Redetermination of Employment Status Under Code Section 7436" and shall contain the following:

(1)   In the case of a petitioner who is an individual, the petitioner's name and State of legal residence; in the case of a petitioner other than an individual, the petitioner's name and principal place of business or principal office or agency; and, in all cases, the petitioner's mailing address. The mailing address, State of legal residence, and principal place of business, or principal office or agency, shall be stated as of the date that the petition is filed.

(2)   If the Commissioner sent by certified or registered mail to the petitioner notice of the Commissioner's determination of matters set forth in Code section 7436(a)(1) and (2), then—

(A)   the date of the notice in respect of which the petition is filed and the city and State of the office of the Internal Revenue Service that issued the notice; and

(B)   as an attachment, a copy of such notice.

(3)   The calendar quarter or quarters for which the de-

termination was made.

(4) Clear and concise assignments of each and every error which the petitioner alleges to have been committed by the Commissioner in the Commissioner's determination of matters set forth in Code section 7436(a)(1) and (2), and in the Commissioner's determination of the proper amount of employment tax. Any issue not raised in the assign- ments of error shall be deemed to be conceded. Each as- signment of error shall be separately lettered.

(5) Clear and concise lettered statements of the facts on which the petitioner bases the assignments of error.

(6) A prayer setting forth the relief sought by the peti- tioner.

(7) The signature, mailing address, and telephone num- ber of each petitioner or each petitioner's counsel, as well as counsel's Tax Court bar number.

A claim for reasonable litigation or administrative costs shall not be included in the petition in an action for redetermina- tion of employment status. For the requirements as to claims for reasonable litigation or administrative costs, see Rule 231.

(c) Small Tax Case Under Code Section 7436(c): For provisions regarding the content of a petition in a small tax case under Code section 7436(c), see Rules 170 through 175.

(d) Filing Fee: The fee for filing a petition for redeter- mination of employment status shall be $60, payable at the time of filing.

RULE 292. REQUEST FOR PLACE OF TRIAL

At the time of filing a petition for redetermination of em- ployment status, the petitioner shall file a request for place of trial in accordance with Rule 140.

RULE 293. OTHER PLEADINGS

(a) Answer: The Commissioner shall file an answer or shall move with respect to the petition within the periods specified in and in accordance with the provisions of Rule 36.

(b) Reply: For provisions relating to the filing of a reply, see Rule 37.

RULE 294. JOINDER OF ISSUE IN ACTION FOR REDETERMINATION OF EMPLOYMENT STATUS

An action for redetermination of employment status under Code section 7436 shall be deemed at issue as provided by Rule 38.

TITLE XXIX LARGE PARTNERSHIP ACTIONS

RULE 300. GENERAL

(a) **Applicability:** The Rules of this Title XXIX set forth the special provisions that apply to actions for readjust- ment of partnership items of large partnerships under Code section 6247 and actions for adjustment of partnership items of large partnerships under Code section 6252. Except as oth- erwise provided in this Title, the other Rules of Practice and Procedure of the Court, to the extent pertinent, are applica- ble to such large partnership actions.

(b) **Definitions:** As used in the Rules in this Title—

(1) The term "large partnership" means an electing large partnership as defined in Code section 775. See Code sec. 6255(a)(1).

(2) A "large partnership action" is either an "action for readjustment of partnership items of a large partnership" under Code section 6247 or an "action for adjustment of partnership items of a large partnership" under Code sec- tion 6252.

(3) The term "partnership item" means any item de- scribed in Code section 6231(a)(3). See Code sec. 6255(a)(2).

(4) The term "partnership adjustment" means any ad- justment in the amount of any partnership item of a large partnership. See Code sec. 6242(d)(1).

(5) The term "designated partner" means the partner or person designated by the large partnership or selected by the Commissioner pursuant to Code section 6255(b)(1).

(6) A "notice of partnership adjustment" is the notice described in Code section 6245(b).

(7) The term "administrative adjustment request" means a request for an administrative adjustment of part- nership items filed by the large partnership under Code section 6251(a).

(c) **Jurisdictional Requirements:** The Court does not have jurisdiction of a large partnership action under this Title unless the following conditions are satisfied:

(1) *Actions for Readjustment of Partnership Items of a Large Partnership:* (A) The Commissioner has issued a notice of partnership adjustment. See Code sec. 6245(b).

(B) A petition for readjustment of partnership items of a large partnership is filed with the Court by the large partnership within the period specified in Code section 6247(a).

(2) *Actions for Adjustment of Partnership Items of a Large Partnership:* (A) The Commissioner has not al- lowed all or some of the adjustments requested in an ad- ministrative adjustment request. See Code sec. 6252(a).

(B) A petition for adjustment of partnership items of a large partnership is filed with the Court by the large partnership subject to the conditions and within the period specified in Code section 6252(b) and (c).

(d) Form and Style of Papers: All papers filed in a large partnership action shall be prepared in the form and style set forth in Rule 23, and the caption shall state the name of the partnership, as for example, ''ABC Partnership, Petitioner''.

RULE 301. COMMENCEMENT OF LARGE PARTNERSHIP ACTION

[1]**(a) Commencement of Action:** A large partnership action shall be commenced by filing a petition with the Court. See Rule 20, relating to the commencement of a case; Rule 22, relating to the place and manner of filing the peti- tion; Rule 32, relating to form of pleadings; Rule 34(e), relat- ing to the number of copies to be filed; and Rule 300(d), relat- ing to the caption of papers.

(b) Content of Petition: Each petition shall be enti- tled either ''Petition for Readjustment of Partnership Items of a Large Partnership under Code Section 6247'' or ''Petition for Adjustment of Partnership Items of a Large Partnership Under Code Section 6252''. Each such petition shall contain the allegations described in paragraph (c) of this Rule, and the allegations described in either paragraph (d) or para- graph (e) of this Rule.

(c) All Petitions: All petitions in large partnership ac- tions shall contain the following:

(1) The name and principal place of business of the large partnership at the time the petition is filed.

(2) The city and State of the office of the Internal Rev- enue Service with which the large partnership's return for the period in controversy was filed.

(3) A separate numbered paragraph setting forth the name and current address of the designated partner.

A claim for reasonable litigation or administrative costs shall not be included in the petition in a large partnership action. For the requirements as to claims for reasonable litigation or administrative costs, see Rule 231.

(d) Petition for Readjustment of Partnership Items of a Large Partnership: In addition to including the in- formation specified in paragraph (c) of this Rule, a petition for readjustment of partnership items of a large partnership shall also contain:

(1) The date of the notice of partnership adjustment and the city and State of the office of the Internal Revenue Service that issued the notice.

(2) The year or years or other periods for which the no- tice of partnership adjustment was issued.

(3) Clear and concise statements of each and every error which the petitioner alleges to have been committed by the Commissioner in the notice of partnership adjust- ment. The

assignments of error shall include issues in re- spect of which the burden of proof is on the Commissioner. Any issues not raised in the assignments of error, or in the assignments of error in any amendment to the petition, shall be deemed to be conceded. Each assignment of error shall be set forth in a separate lettered subparagraph.

(4) Clear and concise lettered statements of the facts on which the petitioner bases the assignments of error, except with respect to those assignments of error as to which the burden of proof is on the Commissioner.

(5) A prayer setting forth relief sought by the peti- tioner.

(6) The signature, mailing address, and telephone number of the petitioner's designated partner or the petitioner's counsel, as well as counsel's Tax Court bar number.

(7) A copy of the notice of partnership adjustment, which shall be appended to the petition, and with which there shall be included so much of any statement accom- panying the notice as is material to the issues raised by the assignments of error. If the notice of partnership adjustment or any accompanying statement incorporates by reference any prior notices, or other material furnished by the Internal Revenue Service, such parts thereof as are material to the assignments of error likewise shall be ap- pended to the petition.

(e) Petition for Adjustment of Partnership Items of a Large Partnership: In addition to including the infor- mation specified in paragraph (c) of this Rule, a petition for adjustment of partnership items of a large partnership shall also contain:

(1) The date that the administrative adjustment re- quest was filed and other proper allegations showing juris- diction in the Court in accordance with the requirements of Code section 6252(b) and (c).

(2) The year or years or other periods to which the ad- ministrative adjustment request relates.

(3) The city and State of the office of the Internal Rev- enue Service with which the administrative adjustment re- quest was filed.

(4) A clear and concise statement describing each part- nership item on the large partnership return that is sought to be changed, and the basis for each such requested change. Each such statement shall be set forth in a sepa- rately lettered subparagraph.

(5) Clear and concise lettered statements of the facts on which the petitioner relies in support of such requested changes in treatment of partnership items.

(6) A prayer setting forth relief sought by the peti- tioner.

(7) The signature, mailing address, and telephone number of the petitioner's designated partner or the petitioner's counsel, as well as counsel's Tax Court bar number.

(8) A copy of the administrative adjustment request shall

be appended to the petition.

(f) Joinder of Parties: (1) *Permissive Joinder:* A separate petition shall be filed with respect to each notice of partnership adjustment issued to separate large partner- ships. However, a single petition for readjustment of partner- ship items of a large partnership or petition for adjustment   of partnership items of a large partnership may be filed seek- ing readjustments or adjustments of partnership items with respect to more than one notice of partnership adjustment or administrative adjustment request if the notices or requests pertain to the same large partnership.

(2) *Severance or Other Orders:* With respect to a case based upon multiple notices of partnership adjustment or administrative adjustment requests, the Court may order a severance and a separate case may be maintained with respect to one or more of such notices or requests whenever it appears to the Court that proceeding separately is in fur- therance of convenience, or to avoid prejudice, or when sep- arate trials will be conducive to expedition or economy.

RULE 302. REQUEST FOR PLACE OF TRIAL

At the time of filing a petition in a large partnership ac- tion, a request for place of trial shall be filed in accordance with Rule 140.

RULE 303. OTHER PLEADINGS

(a) Answer: The Commissioner shall file an answer or shall move with respect to the petition within the periods specified in and in accordance with the provisions of Rule 36.

(b) Reply: For provisions relating to the filing of a reply, see Rule 37.

RULE 304. JOINDER OF ISSUE IN LARGE PARTNERSHIP ACTIONS

A large partnership action shall be deemed at issue as pro- vided by Rule 38.

RULE 305. ACTION FOR ADJUSTMENT OF PARTNERSHIP ITEMS OF LARGE PARTNERSHIP TREATED AS ACTION FOR READJUSTMENT OF PARTNERSHIP ITEMS OF LARGE PARTNERSHIP

If, after the filing of a petition for adjustment of partner- ship items of a large partnership (see Code section 6252(a) and Rule 301(a)) but before the hearing of such petition, the Commissioner mails to the large partnership a notice of part- nership adjustment for the partnership taxable year to which the petition relates, then such petition shall be treated as a petition in an action for readjustment of the partnership

items to which such notice relates. The petitioner, within 90 days after the date on which the notice of partnership adjustment is mailed, shall file an amendment to the petition, set- ting forth every error which the petitioner alleges to have been committed by the Commissioner in the notice of part- nership adjustment, and the facts on which the petitioner bases the assignments of error. A copy of the notice of partnership adjustment shall be appended to the amendment to the petition.

TITLE XXX ACTIONS FOR DECLARATORY JUDGMENT RELATING TO TREATMENT OF ITEMS OTHER THAN PARTNERSHIP ITEMS WITH RESPECT TO AN OVERSHELTERED RETURN

RULE 310. GENERAL

(a) Applicability: The Rules of this Title XXX set forth the provisions which apply to actions for declaratory judg- ment relating to treatment of items other than partnership items with respect to an oversheltered return pursuant to Code section 6234. Except as otherwise provided in this Title, the other Rules of Practice and Procedure of the Court, to the extent pertinent, are applicable to such actions for declara- tory judgment.

(b) Definitions: As used in the Rules in this Title—

(1) An ''oversheltered return action'' means an action for declaratory judgment provided for in Code section 6234 relating to the treatment of items other than partnership items with respect to an oversheltered return.

(2) The term ''partnership item'' means any item de- scribed in Code section 6231(a)(3).

(3) An ''oversheltered return'' means an income tax re- turn which—

(A) shows no taxable income for the taxable year, and

(B) shows a net loss from partnership items. See Code sec. 6234(b).

(4) ''Declaratory judgment'' is the decision of the Court in an oversheltered return action.

(c) Jurisdiction: The Court shall have jurisdiction of an action for declaratory judgment under this Title when the following conditions are satisfied:

(1) The Commissioner has issued a notice of adjust- ment. See Code sec. 6234(a)(3).

(2) A petition for declaratory judgment is filed with the Court within the period specified in Code section 6234(c). See Code sec. 7502.

RU

RULE 311. COMMENCEMENT OF ACTION FOR DECLARATORY JUDGMENT (OVERSHELTERED RETURN)

(a)   Commencement of Action: An action for declara- tory judgment shall be commenced by filing a petition with the Court. See Rule 22, relating to the place and manner of filing the petition, and Rule 32, relating to form of pleadings.

(b)   Content of Petition: A petition filed pursuant to this Rule shall be entitled ''Petition for Declaratory Judg- ment (Oversheltered Return)'' and shall comply with the re- quirements of Rule 34(b), or shall, in the alternative, be sub- stantially in accordance with Form 1 shown in Appendix I, except that ''adjustment'' shall be substituted therein for ''de- ficiency or liability''.

(c)   Filing Fee: The fee for filing a petition for declara- tory judgment shall be $60, payable at the time of filing.

RULE 312. REQUEST FOR PLACE OF TRIAL

At the time of filing a petition for declaratory judgment with respect to an oversheltered return, the petitioner shall   file a request for place of trial in accordance with Rule 140.

RULE 313. OTHER PLEADINGS

(a)   Answer: The Commissioner shall file an answer or shall move with respect to the petition within the periods specified in and in accordance with the provisions of Rule 36.

(b)   Reply: For provisions relating to the filing of a reply, see Rule 37.

RULE 314. JOINDER OF ISSUE IN ACTION FOR DECLARATORY JUDGMENT (OVERSHELTERED RETURN)

An action for declaratory judgment under this Title XXX shall be deemed at issue as provided by Rule 38.

RULE 315. DISPOSITION OF ACTION FOR DECLARATORY JUDGMENT (OVERSHELTERED RETURN)

Disposition of an oversheltered return action generally will be by trial, conducted in accordance with the Rules contained in Title XIV. In addition, an action for declaratory judgment may be decided without a trial in accordance with the Rules contained in Title XII.

RULE 316. ACTION FOR DECLARATORY JUDGMENT (OVERSHELTERED RETURN) TREATED AS DEFICIENCY ACTION

If, after the filing of a petition for declaratory judgment relating to treatment of items other than partnership items with respect to an oversheltered return for a taxable year but before the Court makes a declaration, the treatment of any partnership item for that taxable year is finally determined pursuant to Code section 6234(g)(4), or any such item ceases to be a partnership item pursuant to Code section 6231(b), and as a result of that final determination or cessation, a deficiency can be determined with respect to the items that are the subject of the notice of adjustment, then the notice of adjustment shall be treated as a notice of deficiency under Code section 6212 and the petition shall be treated as a petition in an action brought under Code section 6213. See Code sec. 6234(g)(3).

TITLE XXX ACTIONS FOR DETERMINATION OF RELIEF FROM JOINT AND SEVERAL LIABILITY ON A JOINT RETURN

RULE 320. GENERAL

(a) Applicability: The Rules of this Title XXXI set forth the provisions that apply to actions for the determination of relief from joint and several liability on a joint return pursuant to Code section 6015(e). Except as otherwise provided in this Title, the other Rules of Practice and Procedure of the Court, to the extent pertinent, are applicable to such actions.

(b) Jurisdiction: The Court shall have jurisdiction of an action for determination of relief from joint and several liability on a joint return under this Title when the conditions of Code section 6015(e) have been satisfied.

(c) Form and Style of Papers: All papers filed in an action for determination of relief from joint and several liability on a joint return shall be prepared in the form and style set forth in Rule 23.

RULE 321. COMMENCEMENT OF ACTION FOR DETERMINATION OF RELIEF FROM JOINT AND SEVERAL LIABILITY ON A JOINT RETURN

(a) Commencement of Action: An action for determination of relief from joint and several liability on a joint return is commenced by filing a petition with the Court. See Rule 20, relating to the commencement of a case; Rule 22, relating to the place and manner of filing the petition; and Rule 32, relating to the form of pleadings.

(b) Content of Petition: A petition filed pursuant to this Rule shall be entitled "Petition for Determination of Relief From Joint and Several Liability on a Joint Return" and shall contain the following:

(1)   The petitioner's name, State of legal residence, and mailing address.

(2)   A statement of the facts upon which the petitioner relies to support the jurisdiction of the Court and, as an attachment, a copy of the Commissioner's notice of determination of the relief available pursuant to Code section 6015 or, if the Commissioner has not issued to the peti- tioner a notice of determination of the relief available pur- suant to Code section 6015, a copy of the election for relief filed by the petitioner.

(3)   A statement of the facts upon which the petitioner relies in support of the relief requested.

(4)   A prayer setting forth the relief sought by the petitioner.

(5)   The name and mailing address of the other indi- vidual filing the joint return, if available.

(6)   The signature, mailing address, and telephone number of the petitioner or the petitioner's counsel, as well as counsel's Tax Court bar number.

A claim for reasonable litigation or administrative costs shall not be included in the petition in an action for determination of relief from joint and several liability on a joint return. For the requirements as to claims for reasonable litigation or administrative costs, see Rule 231.

(c)   Small Tax Case Under Code Section 7463(f)(1):   For provisions regarding the content of a petition in a small tax case under Code section 7463(f)(1), see Rules 170 through 175.

(d)   Filing Fee: The fee for filing a petition for determination of relief from joint and several liability on a joint return shall be $60, payable at the time of filing.

RULE 322. REQUEST FOR PLACE OF TRIAL

At the time of filing a petition for determination of relief from joint and several liability on a joint return, the petitioner shall file a request for place of trial in accordance with Rule 140.

RULE 323. OTHER PLEADINGS

(a)   Answer: The Commissioner shall file an answer or shall move with respect to the petition within the periods specified in and in accordance with the provisions of Rule 36.

(b)   Reply: For provisions relating to the filing of a reply, see Rule 37.

RULE 324. JOINDER OF ISSUE IN ACTION FOR DETERMINATION OF RELIEF FROM JOINT AND SEVERAL LIABILITY ON A JOINT RETURN

An action for determination of relief from joint and several liability on a joint return shall be deemed at issue upon the later of:

(1)   The time provided by Rule 38, or

(2)   the expiration of the period within which a notice of intervention may be filed under Rule 325(b).

RULE 325. NOTICE AND INTERVENTION

(a)   Notice: On or before 60 days from the date of the service of the petition, the Commissioner shall serve notice   of the filing of the petition on the other individual filing the joint return and shall simultaneously file with the Court a copy of the notice with an attached certificate of service. The notice shall advise the other individual of the right to inter- vene by filing a notice of intervention with the Court not later than 60 days after the date of service on the other indi- vidual.

(b)   Intervention: If the other individual filing the joint return desires to intervene, then such individual shall file a notice of intervention with the Court not later than 60 days after service of the notice by the Commissioner of the filing   of the petition, unless the Court directs otherwise. All new matters of claim or defense in a notice of intervention shall   be deemed denied. As to the form and content of a notice of intervention, see Appendix I, Form 13.

TITLE XXXII LIEN AND LEVY ACTIONS

RULE 330. GENERAL

(a)   Applicability: The Rules of this Title XXXII set forth the provisions that apply to lien and levy actions under Code sections 6320(c) and 6330(d). Except as otherwise pro- vided in this Title, the other Rules of Practice and Procedure of the Court, to the extent pertinent, are applicable to such actions.

(b)   Jurisdiction: The Court shall have jurisdiction of a lien or levy action under this Title when the conditions of Code section 6320(c) or 6330(d), as applicable, have been sat- isfied.

RULE 331. COMMENCEMENT OF LIEN AND LEVY ACTION

(a)   Commencement of Action: A lien and levy action under Code sections 6320(c) and 6330(d) shall be commenced by filing a petition with the Court. See Rule 20, relating to the commencement of a case; Rule 22, relating to the place and manner of filing the petition; and Rule 32, regarding the form of pleadings.

(b)   Content of Petition: A petition filed pursuant to this

Rule shall be entitled ''Petition for Lien or Levy Action Under Code Section 6320(c) or 6330(d)'', as applicable, and shall contain the following:

(1) In the case of a petitioner who is an individual, the petitioner's name and State of legal residence; in the case of a petitioner other than an individual, the petitioner's name and principal place of business or principal office or agency; and, in all cases, the petitioner's mailing address. The mailing address, State of legal residence, and principal place of business, or principal office or agency, shall be stated as of the date that the petition is filed.

(2) The date of the notice of determination concerning collection action(s) under Code section 6320 and/or 6330 by the Internal Revenue Service Office of Appeals (hereinafter the ''notice of determination''), and the city and State of the Office which made such determination.

(3) The amount or amounts and type of underlying tax liability, and the year or years or other periods to which the notice of determination relates.

(4) Clear and concise assignments of each and every error which the petitioner alleges to have been committed in the notice of determination. Any issue not raised in the assignments of error shall be deemed to be conceded. Each assignment of error shall be separately lettered.

(5) Clear and concise lettered statements of the facts on which the petitioner bases each assignment of error.

(6) A prayer setting forth the relief sought by the petitioner.

(7) The signature, mailing address, and telephone number of each petitioner or each petitioner's counsel, as well as counsel's Tax Court bar number.

(8) As an attachment, a copy of the notice of determination.

A claim for reasonable litigation or administrative costs shall not be included in the petition in a lien and levy action. For the requirements as to claims for reasonable litigation or administrative costs, see Rule 231.

(c) Small Tax Case Under Code Section 7463(f)(2): For provisions regarding the content of a petition in a small tax case under Code section 7463(f)(2), see Rules 170 through 175.

(d) Filing Fee: The fee for filing a petition for a lien and levy action shall be $60, payable at the time of filing.

RULE 332. REQUEST FOR PLACE OF TRIAL

At the time of filing a petition for a lien and levy action, a request for place of trial shall be filed in accordance with Rule 140.

RULE 333. OTHER PLEADINGS

(a) Answer: The Commissioner shall file an answer or shall move with respect to the petition within the periods specified in and in accordance with the provisions of Rule 36.

(b) Reply: For provisions relating to the filing of a reply, see Rule 37.

RULE 334. JOINDER OF ISSUE IN LIEN AND LEVY ACTIONS

A lien and levy action under Code sections 6320(c) and 6330(d) shall be deemed at issue as provided by Rule 38.

TITLE XXXIII
WHISTLEBLOWER ACTIONS

RULE 340. GENERAL

(a) Applicability: The Rules of this Title XXXIII set forth the provisions that apply to whistleblower actions under Code section 7623(b)(4). Except as otherwise provided in this Title, the other Rules of Practice and Procedure of the Court, to the extent pertinent, are applicable to such actions.

(b) Jurisdiction: The Court shall have jurisdiction of a whistleblower action under this Title when the conditions of Code section 7623(b)(4) have been satisfied.

RULE 341. COMMENCEMENT OF WHISTLEBLOWER ACTION

(a) Commencement of Action: A whistleblower action under Code section 7623(b)(4) shall be commenced by filing a petition with the Court. See Rule 20, relating to the commencement of a case; Rule 22, relating to the place and manner of filing the petition; and Rule 32, regarding the form of pleadings.

(b) Content of Petition: A petition filed pursuant to this Rule shall be entitled "Petition for Whistleblower Action Under Code Section 7623(b)(4)" and shall contain the following:

(1) The petitioner's name, State of legal residence, and mailing address, stated as of the date that the petition is filed.

(2) The date of the determination regarding an award under Code section 7623(b)(1), (2), or (3) by the Internal Revenue Service Whistleblower Office.

(3) Lettered statements explaining why the petitioner disagrees with the determination by the Internal Revenue Service Whistleblower Office.

(4) Lettered statements setting forth the facts upon which

the petitioner relies to support the petitioner's posi- tion.

(5) A prayer setting forth the relief sought by the peti-tioner.

(6) The signature, mailing address, and telephone num-ber of each petitioner or each petitioner's counsel, as well as counsel's Tax Court bar number.

(7) As an attachment, a copy of the determination.

(c) Filing Fee: The fee for filing a petition for a whis-tleblower action shall be $60, payable at the time of filing.

RULE 342. REQUEST FOR PLACE OF TRIAL

At the time of filing a petition for a whistleblower action,   a request for place of trial shall be filed in accordance with Rule 140.

RULE 343. OTHER PLEADINGS

(a) Answer: The Commissioner shall file an answer or shall move with respect to the petition within the periods specified in and in accordance with the provisions of Rule 36.

(b) Reply: For provisions relating to the filing of a reply, see Rule 37.

RULE 344. JOINDER OF ISSUE IN WHISTLEBLOWER ACTION

A whistleblower action under Code section 7623(b)(4) shall be deemed at issue as provided by Rule 38.

RULE 345. PRIVACY PROTECTIONS FOR FILINGS IN WHISTLEBLOWER ACTIONS [1]

(a) Anonymous Petitioner: A petitioner in a whistle-blower action may move the Court for permission to proceed anonymously, if appropriate. Unless otherwise permitted by the Court, a petitioner seeking to proceed anonymously pur- suant to this Rule shall file with the petition a motion, with   or without supporting affidavits or declarations, setting forth   a sufficient, fact-specific basis for anonymity. The petition and all other filings shall be temporarily sealed pending a ruling by the Court on the motion to proceed anonymously.

(b) Redacted Filings: Except as otherwise directed by the Court, in an electronic or paper filing with the Court in a whistleblower action, a party or nonparty making the filing shall refrain from including, or shall take appropriate steps   to redact, the name, address, and other identifying informa- tion of the taxpayer to whom the claim relates. The party or nonparty filing a document that contains redacted informa- tion shall file under seal a reference list that identifies each item of redacted information and specifies an appropriate identifier that uniquely corresponds to each item listed. The list may be amended as a matter of right. Subsequent ref- erences in the case to a listed identifier will be construed to refer to the corresponding item of information. The Court in its discretion may later unseal the reference list, in whole or in part, if appropriate.

(c) Other Applicable Rules: For Rules concerned with privacy protections and protective orders, generally, see Rules 27 and 103(a).

APPENDIX I FORMS

The following forms are listed in this appendix:

Form 1. Petition (Sample Format) [1]
Form 2. Petition (Simplified Form) [2]
Form 3. Petition for Administrative Costs (Sec.7430(f)(2))
Form 4. Statement of Taxpayer Identification Number
Form 5. Request for Place of Trial [3]
Form 6. Ownership Disclosure Statement [4]
Form 7. Entry of Appearance
Form 8. Substitution of Counsel
Form 9. Certificate of Service
Form 10. Notice of Change of Address [5]
Form 11. Notice of Election To Intervene
Form 12. Notice of Election To Participate
Form 13. Notice of Intervention [6]
Form 14. Subpoena [7]
Form 15. Application for Order To Take Deposition To Perpetuate Evidence [8]
Form 16. Certificate on Return
Form 17. Notice of Appeal to Court of Appeals
Form 18. Unsworn Declaration Under Penalty of Perjury [9]

All the forms are available on the Court's Web site at *www.ustaxcourt.gov* and upon request from the Clerk of the Court. The forms also may be manually pre- pared, except that the subpoena (Form 14) must be obtained either from the Clerk of the Court or from the Court's Web site. When preparing papers for filing with the Court, attention should be given to the applicable requirements of Rule 23 in regard to form, size, type, and number of copies, as well as to such other Rules of the Court as may apply to the particular item.

[1] The amendment is effective as of May 5, 2011.

[2] The amendments are effective as of May 5, 2011.

[3] The amendments are effective as of September 22, 2010.

[4] New Form 6 is generally effective as of January 1, 2010. The amend- ments addressing petitions filed pursuant to section 6221 et seq. (TEFRA) are effective as of May 5, 2011.

[5] The amendments are effective as of September 18, 2009.

[6] The amendment is effective as of September 18, 2009.

[7] The amendment is effective as of May 5, 2011.

[8] The amendments are effective as of May 5, 2011.

[9] New Form 18 is effective as of July 6, 2012.

FORM 1 PETITION (Sample Format) * (See Rules 30 through 34.)
www.ustaxcourt.gov
UNITED STATES TAX COURT

....

Petitioner(s)

v. Docket No.   #

COMMISSIONER OF INTERNAL REVENUE,

Respondent

PETITION

Petitioner hereby petitions for a redetermination of the deficiency (or liability) set forth by the Commissioner of Internal Revenue in the Commissioner's notice of deficiency (or liability) dated ...., and as the basis for petitioner's case alleges as follows:

1. Petitioner is [set forth whether an individual, corporation, etc., as provided in Rule 60] with mailing address now at

....

    Street (or P.O. Box)   City   State   ZIP Code

and with the State of legal residence (or principal office) now in (if different from the mailing address)

....

The return for the period here involved was filed with the Office of the Internal Revenue Service at ....

                             City   State

2. The notice of deficiency (or liability) was mailed to petitioner on ...., and was issued by the Office of the Internal Revenue Service at ....

                                             City   State

A copy of the notice of deficiency (or liability), including so much of the statement and schedules accompanying the notice as is material, should be redacted as pro- vided by Rule 27 and attached to the petition as Exhibit A. Petitioner must submit with the petition a Form 4, Statement of Taxpayer Identification Number.

3. The deficiencies (or liabilities) as determined by the Commissioner are in in- come (estate, gift, or certain excise) taxes for the calendar (or fiscal) year ...., in the amount of $............., of which $............. is in dispute.

4. The determination of the tax set forth in the said notice of deficiency (or liabil- ity) is based upon the following errors: [Here set forth specifically in lettered sub- paragraphs the assignments of error in a concise manner. Do not plead facts, which properly belong in the succeeding paragraph.]

5. The facts upon which petitioner relies, as the basis of petitioner's case, are as follows: [Here set forth allegations of fact, but not the evidence, sufficient to inform the Court and the Commissioner of the positions taken and the bases therefor. Set forth the allegations in orderly and logical sequence, with subparagraphs lettered,

* Form 1 provides a sample format that is especially appropriate for use by counsel in complex deficiency and liability cases. See Rule 34(a)(1), (b)(1). To adapt Form 1 for use in the following types of actions, see also the applicable Rules, as indicated: Declaratory judgment actions (Rule 211); disclosure actions (Rule 221); partner- ship actions (Rules 241, 301); interest abatement actions (Rule 281); employment status actions (Rule 291); ac- tions for determination of relief from joint and several liability (Rule 321); lien and levy actions (Rule 331); and whistleblower actions (Rule 341). See Form 2 for a fillable form that may be useful for self-represented peti- tioners and may also be used by counsel in simple cases with limited issues. See Form 3 for a fillable form that may be used for administrative costs actions.

so as to enable the Commissioner to admit or deny each allegation. See Rules 31(a) and 34(b)(5).]

WHEREFORE, petitioner prays that [here set forth the relief desired].

                          (Signed) ....

                                         Petitioner or Counsel

                                ....

                                    Present Address—City, State, ZIP Code

Dated: ....

                                    (Area Code) Telephone No.

                                ....

                                    Counsel's Tax Court Bar Number

FORM 2 PETITION (Simplified Form) UNITED STATES TAX COURT

www.ustaxcourt.gov

(FIRST) (MIDDLE) (LAST)

....

(PLEASE TYPE OR PRINT)   Petitioner(s)

            v. Docket No.   #

COMMISSIONER OF INTERNAL REVENUE,

                Respondent

PETITION

1. Please check the appropriate box(es) to show which IRS NOTICE(S) you dispute:

b Notice of Deficiency

b Notice of Determination Concerning Your Request for Relief From Joint and Several Liability. (If you requested relief from joint and several liability but the IRS has not made a determination, please see the Information for Persons Representing Themselves Before the U.S. Tax Court booklet or the Tax Court's Web site.)

b Notice of Determination Concerning Collection Action

b Notice of Determination of Worker Classification

2. Provide the date(s) the IRS issued the NOTICE(S) checked above and the city and State of the IRS office(s) issuing the NOTICE(S): ....

3. Provide the year(s) or period(s) for which the NOTICE(S) was/were issued: ....

4. SELECT ONE OF THE FOLLOWING:

If you want your case conducted under small tax case procedures, check here: b (CHECK

If you want your case conducted under regular tax case procedures, check here: bONE BOX)

NOTE: A decision in a "small tax case" cannot be appealed to a Court of Appeals by the taxpayer or the IRS. If you do not check either box, the Court will file your case as a regular tax case.

5. Explain why you disagree with the IRS determination in this case (please list each point separately):

....
....
....
....
....
....

6. State the facts upon which you rely (please list each point separately):

....
....
....
....
....
....

You may use additional pages to explain why you disagree with the IRS determination or to state additional facts. Please do not submit tax forms, receipts, or other types of evidence with this petition.

ENCLOSURES:

Please check the appropriate boxes to show that you have enclosed the following items with this petition:

b A copy of the NOTICE(S) the IRS issued to you

b The Statement of Taxpayer Identification Number (Form 4) (See PRIVACY NOTICE below.)

b The Request for Place of Trial (Form 5)   b The filing fee

PRIVACY NOTICE: Form 4 (Statement of Taxpayer Identification Number) will *not* be part of the Court's public files. All other documents filed with the Court, in- cluding this Petition and any IRS Notice that you enclose with this Petition, will become part of the Court's public files. To protect your privacy, you are *strongly* en- couraged to omit or remove from this Petition, from any enclosed IRS Notice, and from any other document (other than Form 4) your taxpayer identification number (e.g., your Social Security number) and certain other confidential information as specified in the Tax Court's ''Notice Regarding Privacy and Public Access to Case Files'', available at *www.ustaxcourt.gov.*

....

Signature of Petitioner   Date   (Area Code) Telephone No.

....

Mailing Address   City, State, ZIP Code

State of legal residence (if different from the mailing address):

....

....

Signature of Additional Petitioner (e.g.,Spouse) Date   (Area Code) Telephone No.

....

Mailing Address   City, State, ZIP Code

State of legal residence (if different from the mailing address):

....

....

Signature, Name, Address, Telephone No., and Tax Court Bar No. of Counsel, if retained by Petitioner(s)

SAMPLE

Information About Filing a Case in the United States Tax Court

Attached are the forms to use in filing your case in the United States Tax Court. It is very important that you take time to carefully read the information on this page and that you properly complete and submit these forms to the United States Tax Court, 400 Second Street, N.W., Washington, D.C. 20217.

Small Tax Case or Regular Tax Case

If you seek review of one of the four types of IRS Notices listed in paragraph 1 of the petition form (Form 2), you may file your petition as a ''small tax case'' if your dispute meets certain dollar limits (described below). ''Small tax cases'' are handled under simpler, less formal procedures than regular cases. However, the Tax Court's decision in a small tax case *cannot be appealed* to a Court of Appeals by the IRS or by the taxpayer(s).

You can choose to have your case conducted as either a small tax case or a regular case by checking the appropriate box in paragraph 4 of the petition form (Form 2). If you check neither box, the Court will file your case as a regular case.

Dollar Limits: Dollar limits for a small tax case vary slightly depending on the type of IRS action you seek to have the Tax Court review:

(1) If you seek review of an IRS Notice of Deficiency, the amount of the deficiency (including any additions to tax or penalties) that you dispute cannot exceed $50,000 for any year.

(2) If you seek review of an IRS Notice of Determination Concerning Collection Action, the total amount of unpaid tax cannot exceed $50,000 for all years combined.

(3) If you seek review of an IRS Notice of Determination Concerning Your Request for Relief From Joint and Several Liability (or if the IRS failed to send you any Notice of Determination with respect to a request for spousal relief that you submitted to the IRS at least 6 months ago), the amount of spousal relief sought cannot exceed $50,000 for all years combined.

(4) If you seek review of an IRS Notice of Determination of Worker Classification, the amount in dispute cannot exceed $50,000 for any calendar quarter.

Enclosures

To help ensure that your case is properly processed, please enclose the following items when you mail your petition to the Tax Court:

1. A copy of the Notice of Deficiency or Notice of Determination the IRS sent you;
2. Your Statement of Taxpayer Identification Number (Form 4);
3. The Request for Place of Trial (Form 5); and
4. The $60 filing fee, payable by check, money order, or other draft, to the ''Clerk, United States Tax Court''; or, if applicable, the fee waiver form.

For further important information, see the Court's Web site at *www.ustaxcourt.gov* or the ''Information for Persons Representing Themselves Be- fore the U.S. Tax Court'' booklet available from the Tax Court.

FORM 3 PETITION FOR ADMINISTRATIVE COSTS (SEC. 7430(f)(2))

(See Rules 270 through 274.)

www.ustaxcourt.gov

UNITED STATES TAX COURT

....
Petitioner(s)
v. Docket No.   #
COMMISSIONER OF INTERNAL REVENUE,
Respondent

PETITION FOR ADMINISTRATIVE COSTS
(Sec. 7430(f)(2))

1.   Petitioner(s) appeal(s) the DECISION dated .... denying (in whole or in part) an award for reasonable administrative costs by the Internal Rev- enue Service. A copy of the DECISION should be redacted as provided by Rule 27   and attached to the petition. You must submit with the petition a Form 4, State- ment of Taxpayer Identification Number.

2.   Set forth in the appropriate column the AMOUNT of administrative costs (a) claimed in the administrative proceeding, (b) denied by the Internal Revenue Serv- ice, and (c) now claimed in this Court proceeding (if different from the amount claimed in the administrative proceeding).

(a) Claimed	(b) Denied	(c) Now claimed
$	$	$

3.   Explain briefly why you disagree with the DECISION denying an award for reasonable administrative costs by the Internal Revenue Service.

....
....
....
....

4.   Petitioner(s)' present net worth (does) (does not) exceed $2,000,000. [Strike through as appropriate.]

....
Signature of Petitioner   Date   Signature of Petitioner (Spouse)   Date
....
Present Address—City, State, ZIP Code, Telephone No. (including Area Code)
....
Signature of counsel (if retained by petitioners)   Date
....
Name, Address, Telephone No. (including Area Code), and Tax Court Bar No. of Counsel

FORM 4 STATEMENT OF TAXPAYER IDENTIFICATION NUMBER

(See Rule 20(b).)

www.ustaxcourt.gov

UNITED STATES TAX COURT

....
Petitioner(s)
v. Docket No.   #
COMMISSIONER OF INTERNAL REVENUE,
Respondent

STATEMENT OF TAXPAYER IDENTIFICATION NUMBER
(E.g., Social Security number(s), employer identification number(s))

Name of Petitioner ....
Petitioner's Taxpayer Identification Number ....
Name of Additional Petitioner ....
Additional Petitioner's Taxpayer Identification Number ....

If either petitioner is seeking relief from joint and several liability on a joint re- turn pursuant to Section 6015, I.R.C. 1986, and Rules 320 through 325, name of the other individual with whom petitioner filed a joint return .... Taxpayer Identification Number of the other individual, if available

....

....
Signature of Petitioner or Counsel   Date

....
Signature of Additional Petitioner   Date

FORM 5—REQUEST FOR PLACE OF TRIAL

(See Rule 140.)

www.ustaxcourt.gov

UNITED STATES TAX COURT

....

Petitioner(s)

v. Docket No.   #

COMMISSIONER OF INTERNAL REVENUE,

Respondent

REQUEST FOR PLACE OF TRIAL

PLACE AN X IN ONE BOX. REQUEST A CITY MARKED * ONLY IF YOU ELECTED SMALL TAX CASE STATUS ON FORM 2. ANY OTHER CITY MAY BE REQUESTED FOR ANY CASE, INCLUDING A SMALL TAX CASE.

ALABAMA
   b Birmingham
   b Mobile ALASKA
   b Anchorage ARIZONA
   b Phoenix ARKANSAS
   b Little Rock CALIFORNIA
   b Fresno*
   b Los Angeles
   b San Diego
   b San Francisco COLORADO
   b Denver CONNECTICUT
   b Hartford DISTRICT OF
      COLUMBIA
   b Washington FLORIDA
   b Jacksonville
   b Miami
   b Tallahassee*
   b Tampa GEORGIA
   b Atlanta HAWAII
   b Honolulu IDAHO
   b Boise
   b Pocatello* ILLINOIS
   b Chicago
   b Peoria* INDIANA
   b Indianapolis IOWA
   b Des Moines

KANSAS
   b Wichita* KENTUCKY
   b Louisville LOUISIANA
   b New Orleans
   b Shreveport* MAINE
   b Portland* MARYLAND
   b Baltimore MASSACHUSETTS
   b Boston MICHIGAN
   b Detroit MINNESOTA
   b St. Paul MISSISSIPPI
   b Jackson MISSOURI
   b Kansas City
   b St. Louis MONTANA
   b Billings*
   b Helena NEBRASKA
   b Omaha NEVADA
   b Las Vegas
   b Reno
NEW MEXICO
   b Albuquerque NEW YORK
   b Albany*
   b Buffalo
   b New York City
   b Syracuse* NORTH CAROLINA
   b Winston-Salem NORTH DAKOTA
   b Bismarck*

OHIO
   b Cincinnati b Cleveland b Columbus

173

OKLAHOMA
   ƀ Oklahoma City OREGON
   ƀ Portland PENNSYLVANIA
   ƀ Philadelphia
   ƀ Pittsburgh SOUTH CAROLINA
   ƀ Columbia SOUTH DAKOTA
   ƀ Aberdeen* TENNESSEE
   ƀ Knoxville ƀ Memphis ƀ Nashville
TEXAS
   ƀ Dallas ƀ El Paso ƀ Houston ƀ Lubbock
   ƀ San Antonio UTAH
   ƀ Salt Lake City VERMONT
   ƀ Burlington* VIRGINIA
   ƀ Richmond
   ƀ Roanoke* WASHINGTON
   ƀ Seattle
   ƀ Spokane WEST VIRGINIA
   ƀ Charleston WISCONSIN
   ƀ Milwaukee WYOMING
   ƀ Cheyenne*

....
Signature of Petitioner(s) or Counsel   Date

FORM 6 OWNERSHIP DISCLOSURE STATEMENT

(See Rule 20(c).)

www.ustaxcourt.gov

UNITED STATES TAX COURT

....
Petitioner(s)

v. Docket No.   #

COMMISSIONER OF INTERNAL REVENUE,

Respondent

OWNERSHIP DISCLOSURE STATEMENT

Pursuant to Rule 20(c), Tax Court Rules of Practice and Procedure, [Name of Petitioner], makes the following disclosure:

[If petitioner is a nongovernmental corporation, provide the following informa- tion:]

A.   All parent corporations, if any, of petitioner, or state that there are no par- ent corporations:

B.   All publicly held entities owning 10 percent or more of petitioner's stock,   or state that there is no such entity:

OR

[If petitioner is a nongovernmental large partnership or limited liability company, or a tax matters partner or a partner other than a tax matters partner of a non- governmental partnership, provide the following information:]

All publicly held entities owning an interest in the large partnership, the limited liability company, or the partnership, or state that there is no such entity:

....
Signature of Counsel or Petitioner's   Date
Duly Authorized Representative

175

FORM 7 ENTRY OF APPEARANCE

(See Rule 24.)

www.ustaxcourt.gov

UNITED STATES TAX COURT

....
Petitioner(s)

v. Docket No.   #

COMMISSIONER OF INTERNAL REVENUE,
Respondent

ENTRY OF APPEARANCE

The undersigned, being duly admitted to practice before the United States Tax Court, hereby enters an appearance for the petitioner in the above-entitled case.

Dated: ....
Signature

....
Printed Name

....
Office Address

....
City   State / ZIP Code

....
(Area Code) Telephone No.

....
Tax Court Bar No.

A SEPARATE ENTRY OF APPEARANCE MUST BE FILED IN DUPLICATE FOR EACH DOCKET NUMBER.

FORM 8 SUBSTITUTION OF COUNSEL

(See Rule 24.)

www.ustaxcourt.gov

UNITED STATES TAX COURT

....
Petitioner(s)

v. Docket No.   #

COMMISSIONER OF INTERNAL REVENUE,
Respondent

SUBSTITUTION OF COUNSEL

The undersigned, being duly admitted to practice before the United States Tax Court, hereby enters an appearance for petitioner(s) in the above-entitled case.

Dated: ....
Signature

....
Printed Name

....
Office Address

....
City   State / ZIPCode

....
(Area Code) Telephone No.

....
Tax Court Bar No.

The undersigned hereby withdraws as counsel for petitioner(s) in the above-enti- tled case. Notice of the substitution of the above-named counsel has been given to petitioner(s) and/or counsel for petitioner(s) and to each of the other parties to the case or their counsel, and no party objects to the substitution and withdrawal.

Dated: ....
Signature

....
Printed Name

FORM 9 CERTIFICATE OF SERVICE

(See Rule 21(b)(1).)

www.ustaxcourt.gov

This is to certify that a copy of the foregoing paper was served on .... by (delivering the same to .... at .... on ....) or (mailing the same on .... in a postage-paid wrapper addressed to .... at ....).

Dated: ....
Party or Counsel

(7/6/12)   223

FORM 10 NOTICE OF CHANGE OF ADDRESS
(See Rule 21(b)(4).)
www.ustaxcourt.gov

UNITED STATES TAX COURT

....

Petitioner(s)

v. Docket No.   #

COMMISSIONER OF INTERNAL REVENUE,

Respondent

NOTICE OF CHANGE OF ADDRESS
(See Rule 21(b)(4).) *

Please change my/our address on the records of the Court.

Old Address:

Signature: _____

Printed Name: _____

Tax Court Bar No. (if applicable):

_____

Date: _____

* See also Rule 200(e), which requires each person admitted to practice before the Tax Court promptly to no- tify the Admissions Clerk of any change in office address for mailing purposes. Filing Form 10 in a pending   case satisfies this requirement. If a practitioner has not entered an appearance in a pending case, the practi-   tioner can satisfy the Rule 200(e) notification requirement by mailing Form 10 (omitting any caption and docket number) or other written communication to the Admissions Clerk, or electronically updating the practi- tioner's registration information by clicking on the 'Update Info' tab or link through "Practitioner Access" on the Court's Internet Web site at *www.ustaxcourt.gov.*

Telephone:

New Address:

FORM 11 NOTICE OF ELECTION TO INTERVENE

(Action for Readjustment of Partnership Items)

(See Rule 245.)

www.ustaxcourt.gov

UNITED STATES TAX COURT

ABC Partnership, Richard Roe,
A Partner Other Than the Tax
Matters Partner,
Petitioner
v. Docket No.   #
COMMISSIONER OF INTERNAL REVENUE,
Respondent

NOTICE OF ELECTION TO INTERVENE

Mary Doe, the tax matters partner in the ABC Partnership, hereby elects to intervene, pursuant to section 6226(b)(5), I.R.C. 1986, and Rule 245(a), Tax Court Rules of Practice and Procedure, in the above-entitled action for readjustment of partner- ship items.

Dated: ....

Mary Doe
Tax Matters Partner
Present Address—City, State,
ZIP Code, Telephone No.
(including Area Code)

Dated: ....

Counsel for Tax Matters Partner
Present Address—City, State,
ZIP Code, Telephone No.
(including Area Code)
Tax Court Bar No.

FORM 12 NOTICE OF ELECTION TO PARTICIPATE

(Action for Readjustment of Partnership Items)

(See Rule 245.)

www.ustaxcourt.gov

UNITED STATES TAX COURT

ABC Partnership, Mary Doe,
Tax Matters Partner,
Petitioner
v. Docket No.   #
COMMISSIONER OF INTERNAL REVENUE,
Respondent

NOTICE OF ELECTION TO PARTICIPATE

Richard Roe hereby elects to participate, pursuant to section 6226(c)(2), I.R.C. 1986, and Rule 245(b), Tax Court Rules of Practice and Procedure, in the above-enti- tled action for readjustment of partnership items.

Richard Roe satisfies the requirements of section 6226(d), I.R.C. 1986, because he was a partner during the applicable period(s) for which readjustment of partnership items is sought and, if such readjustment is made, the tax attributable to such part- nership items may be assessed against him.

Dated: ....

Richard Roe
Present Address—City, State,
ZIP Code, Telephone No.
(including Area Code)

Dated: ....

Counsel for Richard Roe
Present Address—City, State,
ZIP Code, Telephone No.
(including Area Code)
Tax Court Bar No.

181

FORM 13 NOTICE OF INTERVENTION

(Action for Determination of Relief From Joint and Several Liability on a Joint Return)

(See Rule 325.)

www.ustaxcourt.gov

UNITED STATES TAX COURT

....
        Petitioner(s)
                    v. Docket No.   #
Commissioner of Internal Revenue,
                    Respondent

NOTICE OF INTERVENTION

Intervenor, ..., the spouse or former spouse of petitioner,
        (Please type or print name.)
hereby intervenes, pursuant to section 6015(e)(4), I.R.C. 1986, and Rule 325, Tax Court Rules of Practice and Procedure, in the above-entitled action.

The grounds for my intervention and reasons why I agree or disagree with the Petition for Determination of Relief From Joint and Several Liability on a Joint Re- turn served on me by respondent, are as follows:

....
....
....
....
....

Dated: ....
                                    Intervenor
                                    Present Address–City, State,
                                    ZIP Code, Telephone No.
                                    (including Area Code)

Dated: ....
                                    Counsel for Intervenor
                                    Present Address–City, State,
                                    ZIP Code, Telephone No.
                                    (including Area Code)
                                    Tax Court Bar No.

FORM 14 SUBPOENA

(See Rule 147)
www.ustaxcourt.gov

UNITED STATES TAX COURT

....
Petitioner(s)

v. Docket No.   #

COMMISSIONER OF INTERNAL REVENUE,

Respondent

SUBPOENA

To ....
....

YOU ARE HEREBY COMMANDED to appear before the United States Tax Court
....
(or the name and official title of a person authorized to take depositions)

at .... on the .... day of ...., ... at ....
    Time   Date   Month   Year

....
Place

then and there to testify on behalf of ....
Petitioner or Respondent

in the above-entitled case, and to bring with you ....
....
....
Use reverse if necessary

and not to depart without leave of the Court.

Date: ....

.... /s/ Robert R. Di Trolio
Attorney for (Petitioner)(Respondent)   Clerk of the Court

===

Return on Service

The above-named witness was summoned on .... at .... by
                                                        Date   Time

delivering a copy of this subpoena to (him)(her), and, if a witness for the petitioner, by
tendering fees and mileage to (him)(her) pursuant to Rule 148 of the Rules of Practice
and Procedure of the Tax Court.

Dated..................................... Signed ....

Subscribed and sworn to before me this .... day of ...., ...

....[Seal]
Name   Titl

FORM 15 APPLICATION FOR ORDER TO TAKE DEPOSITION TO PERPETUATE EVIDENCE

(See Rules 81 through 84.)
www.ustaxcourt.gov
UNITED STATES TAX COURT

....
Petitioner(s)
v. Docket No.   #
COMMISSIONER OF INTERNAL REVENUE,
Respondent

APPLICATION FOR ORDER TO TAKE DEPOSITION TO PERPETUATE EVIDENCE *

To the United States Tax Court:

1. Application is hereby made by the above-named ....
Petitioner or Respondent

for an order to take the deposition(s) of the following named person(s) who has (have) been served with a copy of this application, as evidenced by the attached cer- tificate of service:

Name of witness	Post office address
(a)	....
(b)	....
(c)	....
(d)	....

2. It is desired to take the deposition(s) of the above-named person(s) for the following reasons [With respect to each of the above-named persons, set forth the reasons for taking the depositions rather than waiting until trial to introduce the testi- mony or other evidence.]:

3. The substance of the testimony, to be obtained through the deposition(s), is as follows [With respect to each of the above-named persons, set forth briefly the substance of the expected testimony or other evidence.]:

4. The books, papers, documents, electronically stored information, or other tangible things to be produced at the deposition, are as follows [With respect to each of the above-named persons, describe briefly all things which the applicant desires to have produced at the deposition.]:

5. The expected testimony or other evidence is material to one or more matters in controversy, in the following respects:

6. (a) This deposition (will) (will not) be taken on written questions. See Rule 84.

    (b) All such written questions are annexed to this application [attach such questions pursuant to Rule 84].

7. The petition in this case was filed with the Court on ....
Date

The pleadings in this case (are) (are not) closed. This case (has) (has not) been placed on a trial calendar.

   * An application for an order to take a deposition to perpetuate evidence must be filed at least 45 days prior to the date set for the trial. When the applicant seeks to take depositions upon written questions, the title of the application shall so indicate and the application shall be accompanied by an original and five copies of the proposed questions. The taking of depositions upon written questions is not favored, except when the depositions are to be taken in foreign countries, in which case any depositions taken *must* be upon written questions, except as otherwise directed by the Court for cause shown. (See Rule 84(a).) If the parties so stipulate, depositions may be taken without application to the Court. (See Rule 81(d).) This form may not be used for depositions for discovery purposes, which may be taken only in accordance with Rule 74.

8. An arrangement as to payment of fees and expenses of the deposition is desired which departs from Rules 81(g) and 103, as follows:

....

....

9. It is desired to take the testimony of .... on .... at
Date

.............................., at
Time

....
Room number, street number, street name, city and State

before ....
Name and official title

10. .... is a person who is authorized

184

Name of person before whom deposition is to be taken
to administer an oath, in (his) (her) capacity as ...... Such person is not a relative or employee or counsel of any party, or a relative or employee or associate of such counsel, nor is such person financially interested in the action. (For possible waiver of this requirement, see Rule 81(e)(3).)

11. It is desired to record the testimony of .... before .... by video recording. The name and address of the video recorder operator and the name and address of the operator's employer are ....
....

Dated .... (Signed) ....
                                                                          Petitioner or Counsel

                                        ....
                                                        Post office address

                                        ....
                                                        Counsel's Tax Court Bar No.

FORM 16 CERTIFICATE ON RETURN

(See Rule 81(h).)

www.ustaxcourt.gov

UNITED STATES TAX COURT

....

Petitioner(s)

v. Docket No.   #

COMMISSIONER OF INTERNAL REVENUE,

Respondent

CERTIFICATE ON RETURN OF DEPOSITION

To the United States Tax Court:

I, ..., the person named in an order of this Court dated........................, to take depositions in this case, hereby certify:

1. I proceeded, on ...., at the office of ...., at
             Date

...., at ....o'clock ......m.,
    Room number, street number, street name, city and State

under the said order and in the presence of .... and

...................................., the counsel of the respective parties, to take the following depositions, viz:

...., a witness produced

on behalf of the ....
                    Petitioner or Respondent

...., a witness produced

on behalf of the ....
                    Petitioner or Respondent

...., a witness produced

on behalf of the ....
                    Petitioner or Respondent

2. Each witness was examined under oath at such times and places as conditions of adjournment required, and the testimony of each witness (or each witness's answers to the questions filed) was recorded or otherwise reported and reduced to writing by me or under my direction.

3. After the said testimony of each witness was reduced to writing, the transcript of the testimony was read and signed by the witness and was acknowledged by the witness to be the witness's testimony, in all respects only and correctly transcribed except as otherwise stated.

4. All exhibits introduced during the deposition are transmitted herewith, except to the following extent agreed to by the parties or directed by the Court [state dis- position of exhibits if not transmitted with the deposition]:

5. This deposition (was) (was not) taken on written questions pursuant to Rule 84 of the Rules of Practice and Procedure of the United States Tax Court. All such written questions are annexed to the deposition.

6. After the signing of the deposition, no alterations or changes were made there- in.

7. I am not a relative or employee or counsel of any party, or a relative or em- ployee or associate of such counsel, nor am I financially interested in the action.

....
Signature of person taking deposition

....
Official title

NOTE—This form, when properly executed, should be attached to and bound with the transcript preceding the first page thereof. It should then be delivered to the party taking the deposition or such party's counsel.

(7/6/12)   231

FORM 17 NOTICE OF APPEAL TO COURT OF APPEALS

(See Rules 190 and 191.)

www.ustaxcourt.gov

UNITED STATES TAX COURT

....

Petitioner(s)

v. Docket No.   #

COMMISSIONER OF INTERNAL REVENUE,

Respondent

NOTICE OF APPEAL

Notice is hereby given that ....
hereby appeals to the United States Court of Appeals for the .... Circuit from [that
part of] the decision of this Court entered in the above-captioned proceeding   on the
.... day of .... [relating to ....].

....
Party* or Counsel

....
Post office address

....
Counsel's Tax Court Bar Number

* If husband and wife are parties, then both must sign if both want to appeal.

FORM 18

UNSWORN DECLARATION UNDER PENALTY OF PERJURY

(See 28 U.S.C. sec. 1746.)

www.ustaxcourt.gov

UNITED STATES TAX COURT

....
Petitioner(s)
v. Docket No.   #
COMMISSIONER OF INTERNAL REVENUE,
Respondent

UNSWORN DECLARATION UNDER PENALTY OF PERJURY

I, ..., declare from my personal knowledge that the
[Name]
following facts are true:

[State the facts in as many numbered paragraphs as are needed. Attach additional pages if necessary.]

1. ....
....
....
2. ....
....
....
3. ....
....
....
4. ....
....
....
5. ....
....
....

I declare under penalty of perjury that the foregoing is true and correct. Executed
on ....
[Date]

....
[Signature]

OR

[If the declaration is executed outside of the United States:]

I declare under penalty of perjury under the laws of the United States of America
that the foregoing is true and correct. Executed on ....
[Date]

....
[Signature]

188

APPENDIX II 1 FEES AND CHARGES

(See Rules 148, 190(a), 200(a), and 200(g).)

(a) Fees and Charges Payable to the Court:

1. Filing petition $60.00
2. Application for admission to practice .... *
3. Periodic registration fee .... **
4. Photocopies (plain or certified)—per page 50
5. Certification—per document 5.00
6. Filing notice of appeal .... ***
7. Transmitting record on appeal .... ****

*Amount set by order of the Court (see Rule 200(a)).

**Frequency and amount set by order of the Court (see Rule 200(g)).

***Amount determined in accordance with rule 3(e) of the Federal Rules of Appellate Procedure (see also rules 13 and 14 of such rules).

****Actual cost of insurance and postage.

(b) Charges for Copies of Transcripts of Proceedings:

Transcripts of proceedings before the Tax Court are supplied to the par- ties and to the public by the official reporter at such rates as may be fixed by contract between the Court and the reporter. Information as to those rates may be obtained from the Clerk of the Court or from the trial clerk at a trial session.

1 The amendments are effective as of October 3, 2008.

INDEX

References are to Rule numbers except where specified otherwise.

189

ADMINISTRATIVE COSTS ACTIONS—
  Continued

ADMISSION TO PRACTICE BEFORE COURT   200
(See also PRACTICE BEFORE COURT.)

ADMISSIONS

AFFIDAVITS AND DECLARATIONS

191

194

197

198

199

MOTIONS

MOTIONS—Continued

211

214

215

222

223

ACTION FOR.)

228

TAX COURT RULES OF PRACTICE AND
   PROCEDURE
   (See RULES.)

TAXPAYER IDENTIFICATION NUMBER

TESTIMONY

TIME

TRANSCRIPTS

TRANSFEREES, EXAMINATION BY
   (See also DISCOVERY.)

Made in the USA
Middletown, DE
22 January 2019